# YOU BE NORMAL
# AND I'LL BE ME

*J. C. Auer*

"Witty, charming, clever and moving. An honest narrative of one man's life. Be prepared for an emotional ride."
Marcia Evans

"Auer's unusual style is fractured, innovative, imaginative and yet unpretentious and honest. He is the new voice of his generation."
Michele Fischetti

"I haven't read it yet, but I hear it's good."
T. J. Bailey

*To Mom and Dad*

# TABLE OF CONTENTS

# MOM'S NEW CAR

I would like to tell you a funny story involving my mother. You see, my mother wanted a mink coat for Christmas.

Everyone knew she wanted a mink coat because she was always dropping hints and telling people how much she wanted one. I knew she wanted a mink coat. My dad knew she wanted a mink coat. My sister knew she wanted a mink coat. All of her girlfriends, the milk man, the mailman, the sales lady who put the coat on layaway and even the man who pumped her gas down at the Esso station knew Mom wanted a mink coat.

Christmas morning arrived and we all raced to the Christmas tree to see what Santa Claus had brought us. Dad got me a go-cart! Dad got my sister a bicycle! Dad got my mom a trash compactor! My mother locked herself in their bedroom and cried and cried all day long.

Okay, so that's not the funny part. This is the funny part.

When I was seventeen, my dad gave my mom a car for Christmas. He gave her a brand new 1969 Chevrolet Impala convertible. It was turquoise blue with a white top, blue interior and white wall tires. Mom was absolutely thrilled with her Christmas gift.

Mom loved her new car. She loved looking at it. She loved sitting in it. She loved driving it. She loved putting the top up. She loved taking the top down. She loved it!

I loved boobies. I loved looking at them. I loved trying to peek down girls' blouses in the hope of possibly seeing them. I loved fantasizing that I was taking the top down. I loved boobs!

I kept a carefully concealed collection of mammary magazines in my bedroom. I had a copy of "The National Geographic" showing a topless woman in Africa dancing around while holding a spear. I had the cover from a men's magazine showing a woman dressed in a low-cut Nazi uniform while holding a whip. I also had a copy of the best breast book ever printed, "The Sears Catalog."

The lingerie section of The Sears Catalog was a veritable cornucopia of tantalizing tit photos. It boasted page after page of black and white pictures of women dressed in bras, granny panties and garter belts. I believe most of my many clothing fetishes originated as a result of my masturbating to The Sears Catalog.

One day as I was riding along with my mother in her new car she told me we were on our way to the Greyhound bus station to pick up my cousin Connie. She explained how Connie was going to be attending Concord College in the spring and was coming into town to sign-up for classes.

I explained that I had no interest in riding all the way to Concord College with her and Connie.

As Connie stepped off of the bus I instantly became interested in riding all the way to Concord College with her and Connie. Connie was beautiful. She had big beautiful hair and big beautiful breasts. I liked my cousin Connie.

As we motored along Mom would point out things of interest for Connie to see. I was only interested in seeing Connie's pointy things. Mom told Connie about the town, the college, the Civil War, and the new sewage treatment plant. Then, for reasons which I'll never know, Mom told her about that night's dance at the Memorial Building. She said all the kids would be there and suggested I take Connie to the dance. Connie thought this was a wonderful idea and agreed to go. I was dumbfounded.

At the time, I drove a World War II Army jeep I had customized myself. I'd painted it with red metal-flake paint and covered its aluminum top with paisley orange peel-n-stick shelving paper. It looked awesome, but Mom thought it would be much nicer if I drove Connie to the dance in her car. I was dumbfounded.

I was a fairly good dancer for a white boy. When it came to fast dances, I could do the "Twist" and "The Funky Chicken." I also did this quasi-interpretive hillbilly flatfoot leap around like a fairy dance which impressed the ladies. My slow dancing skills consisted of holding the girl as tight as she would allow while staying in one place and rotating around and around in a clockwise direction.

Connie and I were slow dancing and I was holding her as tight as she would allow and she was allowing me to hold her very tight. Occasionally, I would brush back and forth against her breasts and she didn't back away.

Emboldened, I allowed one of my trembling hands to accidentally slip down and touch her butt and she started kissing me. Right there on the dance floor! Right out in the open! Right there in front of God and everybody, she was kissing me!

Before long we were in the car and driving out to a place where people go "parking." I was taking her to the Boulder Park swimming pool because the area was safe and secluded.

The moment I parked the car we were all over each other. We were making out like banshees and I was doing everything I was supposed to do. I told her she was pretty. I stroked her hair. I sucked on her neck. I put my tongue into her ear. I put my tongue into her mouth. We were "French Kissing"!

Yessiree, Bob! I was doing everything I was supposed to do and it was working. She was hotter than a firecracker and flopping around like a fish out of water. This was it! All I had to do now was to somehow get her top off and her big boobies would be all mine.

In those days, all bra straps were connected to each other by placing some hooks sewn onto the right strap into the holes of some eyelets sewn onto the left strap. To remove one of these bras, a guy needed to possess both knowledge and skill. It required steady hands and nimble fingers. Although I had only "popped a top" once, I knew how it was done.

While distracting the girl with your left hand you would nonchalantly allow your right hand to travel to the back of her blouse or dress. While using your right thumb to hold the bra's eyelets in place you'd take your index finger and push the bra's hooks up, over and out of the eyelet holes, thus unhooking the bra. Ta-Da! It was a "snap."

I was doing everything I was supposed to do and it was working. It was working except for the part where the bra unhooks and flies open. That part wasn't working worth a damn.

Connie's bra had four hooks and, like I said, I had a limited amount of experience opening a bra with two hooks. This bra was way out of my league, but I was not to be denied. I pushed, pinched, pressed and pulled. I clasped those clips and I jammed them together. I rammed them together. I squeezed and scrunched, but struggle as I might, I could not unhook her bra.

As I continued to fumble around like a fool, Connie asked, "Should I take my bra off?" To which I replied, "Would you take your bra off?", whereupon she started to undress.

Now, I had always believed to get a girl's top off you had to somehow trick her. It had never occurred to me that you could ask a girl to take her top off and she would. I was dumbfounded.

The moment her breasts were free and fully exposed, a light shown down from Heaven, bathing the interior of the car in a bright golden glow. It was God's way of saying, "Here's those tits you've been praying for." It was a miracle!

It was not a miracle. It was a street light which had been installed to illuminate the field in which pool patrons parked their cars.

OMG! Her braless bajongas were right there before my eyes and lit up like the Las Vegas strip! This was amazing! I ogled her orbs! I touched her torpedoes! I nibbled her nips! I licked her lactoids! I kissed her kazongas!

OMG! This was awesome! I was doing everything I was supposed to do and it was working. Things were working way better than they had ever worked before. In fact, things were working so well I soon found myself sailing into uncharted waters. I didn't know what I should do.

I didn't know what I should do with Connie, but I knew what I should do with the car. I should move it out from underneath the street light and into a darker, more secluded part of the parking lot before someone drove by and discovered us.

Starting the car, I turned on the headlights. I knew where I was going to go. I had worked at the pool as a life guard and knew the grassy field like the back of my hand. I put the car into "Reverse" and started to slowly back up.

Being as this was a convertible car, it had a clear plastic rear window. Being as we were two hot, half naked teenagers, the plastic window was fogged up to the point where I could not see out of it. So, I cracked my door opened a teeny tiny bit and leaned my head out to see where we were going and BAM!

The bottom edge of the door hit a tree stump, which immediately ripped the door out of my hand, swung it completely around and smashed it into the car's left front quarter panel. I slammed on the brakes! Holy shit! This was bad!

I put the car into "Drive" and eased the door off of the tree stump at which point it fell off of the car and into the field. Holy shit! This was bad!

I put the car into "Park" and Connie put her boobs into her bra. Holy shit! This was bad! This was really, really bad!

Being a man who possessed some mechanical skills, I examined the automobile and concluded there was indeed a great deal of damage done to the car. Being a teenager who had just done a great deal of damage to the car, I began running around and around in the field like a lunatic screaming, "Fuck!" "Shit!" "Damn!" "Boogers!"

Okay, so I never screamed, "Boogers!" but believe me, I was extremely upset nonetheless. I was losing my mind! I was in a frenzy, frantically waving my arms around while shouting profanities and stomping the ground. Connie sat silently, as if in shock.

After talking at Connie for a while I decided it would be best if we got the hell out of there.

In preparation for our departure, I put the top down on the car and the two of us began muscling the damaged door into the backseat.

Now an automobile door when attached to a car is quite easy to move; whereas an automobile door once cleaved from a car is quite difficult to move. This massive mangled metal mess was unmanageable. It was heavy as hell, plus, the car had electric windows so now there was no way to put the window down. This made the door too big and bulky to fit into the back seat.

We tried to put it in the seat, but it wouldn't fit so we had to lift it out and start all over again. We turned it upside down, but it still wouldn't go in so we hauled it out. We'd stand it on this end and it wouldn't fit. We'd stand it on that end and it wouldn't fit. In and out. In and out. We tried every conceivable way to wiggle and worm the door into the back seat, but it refused to go.

By this time, I was becoming somewhat testy and started yelling directions at cousin Connie. She started to cry. Crying is a common reaction many girls have when being screamed at by an asshat.

Connie crawled into the front seat, curled up into a fetal position and began to sob. I felt like shit. I had fucked this up so bad. The car was wrecked, Connie was crying and I was screwed. Any way I looked at it, I was screwed. There was no way out of this mess.

In a moment of madness, I applied the car's tire iron to the door's window. Problem solved! The door would now fit in the rear seat and we were soon on our way.

On the drive back to Concord College not a single word was spoken between us. You could have heard the veritable pin drop if it weren't for the deafening roar of the howling winter wind swirling all around us. The top was down, the door was gone and it was colder than a witch's tit.

Now, I say, "Colder than a witch's tit," without ever having actually touched a witch's tit. At this point the only tits I'd ever touched were Connie's, and I was certain I would never touch them again.

Arriving at the college I dropped Connie off at her dorm. And I mean I literally dropped her off. I pulled up, she got out and I drove away. I should've opened her car door for her and walked her back to her dorm like a gentleman, but I did not. I just ran away like the immature coward I was.

And of course, I should've said something to her. I should have apologized for being such a dickhead and making her cry. I should have apologized for ruining her clothes, for the cut on her hand, and the hickey on her neck.

Yes, as I look back on the evening I have regrets. I should've taken her out to William's farm to go "parking" instead of to Boulder Park pool.

Upon returning home I was physically, mentally and emotionally exhausted. I parked the wretched wreck in the garage and headed straight to my room, tumbled into bed, spent some time with the Sears Catalog, and fell asleep.

The next morning, I was rudely rousted by my mom's voice calling out, "Chris, come on down! Your breakfast is ready!"

Immediately upon awakening I was disappointed to be alive. If I had somehow died in my sleep Jesus would have come and taken me up to Heaven and I wouldn't have to deal with this mess. The idea of having to face my mother filled me with dread and despair.

As I stood in front of the bathroom mirror brushing my teeth and rehearsing my apologies, excuses, and explanations I heard her yelling, "Chris, your breakfast is getting cold! You get down here right now!" I knew my time was up. This was it. I had no choice but to go down and get my comeuppance.

When I sat down at the table Mom asked me, "So how was the dance? Did you guys have fun?" I didn't answer her. I didn't know what say. I wasn't going to lie to her, although I did give the idea some serious consideration. I couldn't answer her so I sat motionless, staring into my bowl of Cream of Wheat.

"So, how was it?" she asked again. And again, I didn't answer her. I didn't know what to say. I didn't know what to do. What should I say? What should I do? What? What? My mind was racing. My heart was pounding. My stomach was churning. The pressure kept building up and up and up inside of me until I exploded.

Bursting from my chair I blurted out "Mom, I'm sorry, but I wrecked your car!" It was as if time itself had stopped. There was no movement and absolute silence until Mom eventually said, "I know, I saw it this morning. I've already talked to Connie's mom."

She walked over and placing a hand on each of my shoulders, looked me in the eye and began to calmly ask some reasonable questions, "Was anyone hurt?" "Did you damage anything else?" "Had you been drinking?" "No Ma'am" was my solemn reply.

My mother wrapped her arms around me and as she kissed me on my forehead she said, "Don't worry, we can get the car fixed. You're okay, that's all that matters."

And that was pretty much it. No drama. No punishment. Just a hug and a kiss. Mom loved her new car, but she loved her son more.

# AVENGING FORCE

In 1986, I was in New Orleans, Louisiana, working on a movie called "Avenging Force." The movie starred Michael Dudikoff and like all of Michael's movies this was a Kung Fu, car chase, blow shit up and burn things down type of movie.

Sharon Mann was the first assistant director and Nancy King was the second assistant director. These two women took me under their wing, took me to New Orleans, and taught me how to properly run a film set.

Sharon would move on to make such major motion pictures as, Top Gun, Terminator 3 and Titanic. Nancy was an assistant director on Alien, Mulholland Falls, and my favorite film, Reform School Girl. It was a privilege and a pleasure to be able to work under these two talented women. However, filmmaking is an intense and pressure-filled occupation and occasionally their nerves would become frayed, their tempers would become short, and my life would become a living hell.

We'd been working fourteen hours a day, six days a week for two consecutive weeks creating and filming an entire Mardi Gras parade. I shit you not, a complete Mardi Gras parade with floats, marching bands, and spectators, plus our parade boasted the extra added attractions of automatic gunfire, explosions, death and destruction.

It was late on a Saturday night and we were working deep below the earth's surface. We were five or six stories down in the ground filming in the New Orleans Civil Defense bomb shelter. The shelter was built in the Fifties as a place where those people with enough money, connections, and political clout could escape Armageddon. If the Communists would happen to start raining nuclear death from above, this was the place where the elite would meet. When the shit hit the fan, this is where the selected few would survive.

We had been down in this abandoned concrete hellhole for well over seven hours. Everyone was tired and testy and Sharon and Nancy were beating on me as if I were a drumhead. They had been riding my ass for hours and I was at the end of my rope. I wanted to tell them both to "Chill out! I'm doing the best I can!" But of course, I could not. I would not, because not only were the two of them my superiors, they were also my friends. They were the ones who had hired me. It was the two of them who had brought me to New Orleans and given me the opportunity to do the job I love to do.

It was roughly thirty minutes until lunch and only seven or eight hours until we'd wrap and start our one day off. I didn't know if I was physically going to make it, but I was certain emotionally I couldn't take another five weeks of this crap. What should I do? How could I tell these two women I was grateful to be working with them, but they needed to mellow out? What to do? What to do?

In a flash, an idea came to me and I knew how I'd handle the situation. I was going to defuse the tensions between us with a practical present, a laugh and a smile.

I contacted a friend in the transportation department and, unbeknownst to the others, I secured a driver and a car to transport me to Bourbon Street. Lunch would last a little over an hour which was enough time for me to complete my mission. I hid in the back seat of a car and as soon as Sharon called out "That's lunch!" my driver and I took off.

After a short scenic drive, we were soon cruising around in one of the seedier sections of town. Searching, searching, searching until I spotted what I was looking for. Eureka! I found it: a porn palace. One-stop shopping for all of your sick sexual needs. "This is the place," I said to the driver. "This is it. Drop me off here." My driver pulled over to the curb, I exited the automobile and walked briskly inside.

The place was dark, dank and deserted except for a rather large black lady who sat behind the counter reading one of those tabloid newspapers. The kind with headlines screaming, "Jackie O is Pregnant, UFOs in Arizona, Rock Hudson is Gay." You know, that type of shit.

She leaped from her seat when I called out, "Where are the vibrators?" Shocked by my sudden appearance she quickly pointed in the direction of a display case filled with various vibrators, dildos, cock rings, and toys.

I knew exactly what I was looking for. It's not like I had never purchased one of these things before. "There's what I want! Give me two of those things!" I exclaimed pointing to one of your standard, every day, basic vibrators. You know the kind. They're six inches long and made of smooth, white plastic. The pointy end is for pleasure and the flat end unscrews so you can put the batteries in it. You twist the top to turn it on and adjust the vibrating speed.

"Would you like to buy some lubricant to go with those?" the large lady asked as she placed my purchase into a poke. "No, thanks," I answered, "but I do need some batteries, don't I?" She grinned at me and said, "Yes, you do honey, but we ain't got no batteries here. You gotta get those from across the street." "What? Are you kidding me?" I said. "No Sir, you gotta get those things across the street," she mumbled from behind her newspaper.

"Well, this sucks," I thought to myself as I exited the porn store only to discover my car was gone. What the hell? The car was gone. The car was gone! I instantly lost my shit!

I began running up and down the street frantically looking for the car like a mad man. "Fuck! Fuck! Fuck!" I kept yelling over and over again as I raced around helter-skelter like an idiot. "Where's the car? Where's the car? WHERE'S THE DAMN CAR?"

Soon, I was reduced to hysterics, screaming at a person who wasn't even there. "When I said, 'Drop me off here,' I didn't mean, 'just drop me off here,' you stupid mother-fucker! I meant, 'Drop me off here and wait on me.' You're supposed to wait on me! Drop me off and wait! You don't just drop me off and leave, you moronic piece of shit! You wait for me! You wait for me, you idiot!"

Now I didn't have a ride back to the film set. I didn't have batteries and I didn't have much time. To make matters worse people were now starting to notice my erratic behavior. Tourists circled me as if I were some type of crazed street performer. They pointed at me and shook their heads.

Realizing these people were watching me and fearing incarceration, I stopped ranting and raving. I smiled and waved as I calmly walked across the street to buy the batteries.

I entered the convenience store like a man on a mission. I needed D-cell batteries and I needed them now! I grabbed a five pack and quickly took my place in the checkout line.

There were only five of us standing there. I checked my watch and I knew I wasn't going to make it back to work in time, but I also knew it was going to be close. I was going to get my batteries, grab a cab, and get my ass back to the set as fast as possible. This was my plan, this was my goal and I was going to make it.

"Let's move along folks, let's move along," I thought to myself as I anxiously watched the checkout girl ring up each purchase. The first customers were a young couple buying a bottle of wine. It looked to me to be a fine Chardonnay with a twist-off top. They paid and walked away. BAM! Now there were only three of us standing in line.

Next up to bat was a zit faced kid. He was buying an RC Cola. "This is going well," I said to myself. I was thinking I'd be out of there soon, but the guy asked to see an issue of Penthouse. The magazine was hidden beneath the counter and I don't even know how he knew the damn thing was down there, but it was. The magazine was stapled shut so he couldn't see what was inside, but he carefully studied the front and back covers for what felt like an eternity before returning it to the cashier. BAM! Now, there were only two of us standing in line.

In front of me was a frail looking Japanese lady and the only thing she was purchasing was a single box of tampons. I checked the time. "Yes, this is going well," I thought to myself. I watched intently as the cashier rang up the tampons and the little lady opened her purse to pay. She pulled some money from her bag, but it was not enough. She took out a little change purse and emptied its contents upon the counter, but alas, she still did not have quite enough to pay for the tampons. Once again, I checked my watch as the lady reached back into her large purse and rooted around in it for spare change. When she pulled out the little change purse for the second time I snapped. I lost it and yelled, "I'll buy the tampons! I'll buy the tampons! Give her the goddamn tampons and I'll pay for them! Okay? I'll buy them!" The cashier jumped back in fright exclaiming, "Okay! Okay Mister!" as the little lady began bowing before me saying, "Thank you. Thank you." BAM! Now I'm the only one standing in line.

Like a Kung Fu master, I slammed my money down onto the counter top. I ripped the vibrators from their boxes, inserted the batteries, grabbed my change and walked briskly out of the store. I stepped out into the street like a Wild West Gunslinger brandishing a loaded vibrator in each of my hands.

Deranged and desperate, I made a beeline straight for the first taxicab I saw. Approaching the driver's side window, I shouted, "I need a cab and I need it now!" The driver was shocked as he turned his head and saw me. I was standing there wide eyed and shaking, snot was running from my nostrils and I was soaked in sweat. I had a thick military belt with a large radio attached to it wrapped around my waist and a headset and microphone on my head. I franticly waved my vibrators in his face as I demanded he take me to the city bomb shelter immediately.

Before he had a chance to think, I jerked opened the back door and jumped in. I assured him I was not dangerous, I was simply having a bad day. I rapidly gave him the Cliff's Notes version as to how I needed to get to the bomb shelter as quickly as possible.

He said he had never heard of the place. I told him it didn't matter; I had a fairly good idea where it was. I said I had lots of money but little time. He said, "What?" I said, "Drive!" and in an instant, we were on our way.

I ordered him to take me to Ponce de Leon Street. "Ponce de Leon! Ponce de Leon!" I kept yelling repeatedly. He said, "What?" I said, "Ponce de Leon! That Fountain of Youth, motherfucker! That Florida dude! Ponce de Leon!" He called out, "Pontchartrain? Pontchartrain? Pontchartrain Boulevard!" "Yes!" I screamed, "Yes! Yes! Yes! Go! Go! Go!"

Soon, we were roaring down Pontchartrain Boulevard, although in what direction I didn't know. I didn't know where I was or where I was going, but I knew I was screwed. I was going to be late and I was going to catch hell for leaving. I should have never left in the first place. I didn't have permission to leave. I had deserted my post during filming, which was much like a soldier deserting his post during battle. I was absolutely going to catch hell. I knew I was screwed. Totally, totally screwed.

Then something wonderful happened. I began hearing intermittent radio chatter coming from the set. We were within radio range of our destination and I experienced an overwhelming sense of newfound confidence.

I contacted the location manager on the QT and told her where I thought we were. She started telling me how to find the location as I carefully relayed her directions to my chauffeur by franticly screaming, "Stop! Turn left! Turnaround! Back up! Back up you fool!" and shit like that.

Eventually, I was clever enough to remove my headset so he could hear her directions directly from the radio. His driving became much faster and more precise as together we raced through the dark of night in search of the shelter.

Somehow, by the grace of God, we reached our destination. I had him turn off his headlights and park a safe distance away so I could enter the area unseen. I shoved a wad of cash through the little window in the partition which separated us and thanked him profusely. I exited the cab and moved quickly for the shelter.

I was late, but if I could slip into the set right away perhaps no one would notice. I was less than a hundred yards from the concrete bunker when I heard a voice cry out, "Wait! Stop! Wait!" I turned around and there stood the cabbie. He was visibly shaking and scared. "What about me?" he asked, "What about me?"

That's when I realized how this poor man had been terrorized by a radio-wearing, fast-talking, vibrator-wielding lunatic. He must have thought this was the end. Everyone was going to die and he didn't want to be left outside of the shelter.

I calmed him as best I could and, against my better judgment, I took him inside. For whatever reason, no one was looking for me or calling for me on the radio. No one asked me where I'd been and the two of us moved freely about the place.

I gave him a tour of the fallout shelter and the movie set before taking him to the craft service table where he joyfully filled up on free coffee and junk food. I escorted him back up to the earth's surface so we could get some fresh air.

We sat there together smoking cigarettes and discussing the evening's adventures. We shared a good laugh and promised each other we'd get together again before I left New Orleans, but of course, we never did.

Back at the hotel, I cleaned up and wrapped up the vibrators. I presented the girls with their gifts and told them how I hoped they would be able to unwind and relax. We shared a good laugh and promised we'd work together again. But of course, we never did.

# WEST VIRGINIA STATE FAIR

Back when I was a young boy, my family would often travel to the West Virginia State Fair. It was a big deal in "The Mountain State."

The State Fair was quite the cultural affair. It boasted hog calling contests! The contestants would say, "Sueeewwwee! Sueeewwwee!" to call the pigs to eat, but the pigs would quite often say, "Thank you so much for the invitation to dine, however, I would prefer to remain lying here in my own feces."

The fair was the place where the state's artisans and farmers would get together once a year to exhibit their talents and skills. They would display their livestock, produce and products and compete with one another for the coveted first place "Blue Ribbon" awarded to the best of the best in each of their chosen fields.

These were intensely competitive and exciting times. West Virginia's farmers would bring the Crème de la Crème of their critters to the fair and compete with one another for the Blue Ribbon prize they all hankered for. Visitors could witness animals such as cows, mules, pigs, sheep and chickens as they gave it their all in their unwavering determination to go for the gold.

There were thrilling exhibitions of homemade creations including, handmade clothes, embroidery, jewelry, quilts, dolls, saddles and bed stands! Beautiful oil paintings and penmanship were on display! There were also culinary competitions to determine who made the most delicious pies, cakes, jellies and jams. And, as if this weren't exciting enough, each and every day was capped off with a live country music concert and a fireworks display.

The Fair also boasted something called the "Midway." As a youngster, my inauguration to the State Fair's Midway was every bit as electrifying as the first time I visited the Las Vegas strip with a head full of acid. It was colorful, chaotic, and crazy.

The Midway was lined with terrifying amusement rides that caused men's sphincters to tighten and women to miscarry. Carnival rides with names such as, "The Himalayan," "The Scrambler," "Crazy Cups," and "The Bullet."

Now, although my younger sister enjoyed riding any and all of these mobile death machines, I was way too much of a "chickenshit-candyass-coward" to even go near them. I once rode the Merry-Go-Round with my Mother and crapped my pants. I'd rather get a vaccination shot than get on a carnival ride. I feared and hated them all, except for the "Round Up."

The Round Up was a rather large ride consisting of a circular horizontal platform with a vertical cage-like wall around its edge. The outside wall had little, open indentations in which its victims would stand side by side. When the ride would start the big wheel would begin to rotate around and around. It would spin faster and faster until the spinning motion would produce enough centrifugal force to push people up against its outer wall.

The outward centrifugal force produced by the spinning wheel made it difficult for the riders to move their arms or legs and they would travel around and around squealing and laughing like the morons they were.

Once the whirling wheel had reached its maximum momentum something truly amazing would occur. The entire fucker filled with fools would tilt up onto its side! I loved the Round Up!

Of course, there was no way in hell I was ever going to get on the contraption, but I was totally entertained watching the mentally challenged riders as they traveled around and around. I enjoyed seeing the panic-stricken looks on their faces and listening to their terrified screams.

I'd stand there mesmerized and praying someone would lose their lunch and blow a big bright chunky rainbow all over the other rotating riders. I had heard many exciting stories of puking passengers and colon explosions, but was never fortunate enough to witness this for myself.

As I write this, West Virginia is rated number one in the nation for obesity, diabetes, heart attack, high blood pressure, cancer, and depression. I now realize the carnival rides were not as dangerous or deadly as the foods I consumed at the fair.

Mountaineers will fry anything. My mother would actually fry apples. She'd melt a stick of butter in a large cast-iron skillet, stir in some cinnamon sugar and add slices of wholesome, healthy, green apples to it. By serving the fried apples with fried pork-chops, fried hush puppies, and a salad containing fried bacon bits she would create a delectably delicious, diabetes-producing, artery-clogging dinner.

Yes, we West Virginians have no fear of dangerous foods and as a youngster I was happy to consume any and all of the dietary delights available at the Fair. I loved them all.

First and foremost were the corn dogs. Valleydale Meats would grind up the ears, guts, lips and assholes of pigs to produce perfect, mouthwatering hot dogs. These wonderful wieners were stuck onto a stick, slathered in cornmeal batter and deep fried in a vat of vegetable oil. I'd eat as many corn dogs as I could coerce my parents into buying. However, today I realize the wooden stick was probably the healthiest part of this frighteningly fatty heart stopper.

Although it consisted mostly of air, I thought cotton candy was cool. It was a pink colored cobweb of pure sugar spun on to a cardboard cone. If you were looking for a quick sugar high, cotton candy was king.

There was a superabundance of sugary substances to snack on at the fair. The donuts were delicious because they combined the basic goodness of deep fried fatty dough covered with your choice of glazed sugar, powdered sugar, or chocolate sugar. There were sugar coated candy caramel apples on a stick. The snow cones were made by covering shaved ice with artificially flavored sugar syrup. A "Pixy Styx" was colored sugar served in a paper straw. And, of course, you can't have a state fair without cookies, cakes, pies, jellies, jams, preserves, soda pop, and ice cream.

In addition to obesity, diabetes, and high blood pressure, West Virginia is also rated number one in the nation for dental disease, boasting the highest rate of all the states for missing teeth. Approximately forty percent of the state's retirees have none of their natural teeth remaining. Many of its children have infected gums and rotting teeth from what is known as, "Mountain Dew Mouth."

While discovering dangerous and damaging foods I was also exposed to a nefarious activity which has brought much pain and suffering into my life.

Like most addictions, it all started innocently enough. I was merely hanging out next to a water trough watching these little yellow rubber ducks float by. They were bobbing up and down and all around when the kid next to me plucked a duck. She reached in and pulled one of these adorable little creatures out of the water, turned it upside down, and lo and behold it had a red number on its ass.

Next thing I know she is leaping around like a lunatic screaming "Winner! Winner!" and an old man gives her a stuffed bear. A little boy grabs a duck and the old man gives him a plastic sword. So, I reach in and pull out a duck and the old man rips the duck out of my hand and doesn't give me a damn thing. WTF?

I learned you have to "pay to play" and this is when my gambling problems first began.

Before I knew it, I was addicted to ducks. I was hooked on this game of chance and shamelessly begged money from my parents. However, I soon became restless as the suspense and excitement of plucking a duck no longer satisfied me.

I began searching around the Midway for a higher stakes game to play. I soon found myself tossing dimes at dishes. I'd graduated from ducks to dishes.

Flinging dimes at dishes is a long odds game. It's much more difficult than plucking ducks and I sucked at it. I was literally throwing my money away. I wasn't having any fun, and yet, I felt compelled to continue playing.

This was risky business and in a short time I was down to my last dime. My final dime and I was going to lay it all on the line. So, holding the last of my cash between two fingers, I said a short prayer and let 'er fly. I knew it was a long shot, but I took that final chance and I won. Yes! I did it! I was a winner!

I was the recipient of a decorative cake plate! With a triumphant smile upon my face I proudly paraded around the fairgrounds displaying my prize plate for all to see. I was no longer an innocent child. I was now a gambler.

As I write this I'm reminded of the many joy-filled days I spent at the West Virginia State Fair. The sight of the large crowds wandering aimlessly throughout the fairgrounds, the sweet smells wafting in the breeze from fat fryers, animal feces, and diesel fuel. The sounds of the fairgrounds are forever etched in my mind: music playing, children laughing and a carnival barker singing out, "She walks! She talks! She crawls on her belly like a reptile!"

"She walks! She talks! She crawls on her belly like a reptile!" are magical words that changed my life. For these are the words which directed my attention to a giant poster depicting Shika!

Shika was a vivacious South Pacific beauty with long black hair flowing seductively over her bare breasts. She was fashionably attired in a grass skirt and looked utterly ravishing as she stood there elegantly surrounded by venomous reptiles and rats. She was dining on the bloody arm she had torn from the body of a dead sailor. Hubba, hubba!

Yes, Shika was a hottie. She was my type of woman and her image was instantly burned deep into my sexual psyche! I felt faint as the blood rushed from my brain and flooded into my pubescent penis.

I didn't care about the rats and reptiles. I didn't care she dined on dead sailors. All I cared about was she was topless and her bountiful breasts were bigger than my head. I was in love! I'd never wanted any woman so much in my life. In fact, at my age I'd never wanted ANY woman in my life.

Love is immortal and my love for Shika would have lasted for all eternity if I hadn't been distracted by a cow with five legs. I witnessed a mad menagerie of deformed animals such as two-headed calves, three-legged sheep, dwarf miniature horses, giant rats, deadly piranhas and two-headed turtles! I was filled with a sense of awe and delight!

And then, when I thought my young life couldn't possibly get any better, it did! I discovered a wide variety of humans with all types of deformities and diseases. People sporting multiple arms, legs and heads. There were tiny little people, extremely tall people, skinny people, obese people, hairy people, and dead people. These were Geeks and Freaks.

These were my people! "Mule-Faced Woman" (facial tumors), "Frog Boy" (guy with an extended stomach, spindly legs and wearing green tights), "Alligator Woman" (ichthyosis), "Lobster Boy," (ectrodactyl), "The Human Pincushion" (sticks needles through his flesh), "The Human Blockhead" (hammers nails up his nose), "Seal Boy" (runs around barking and flapping his vestigial hands), and "The Tattooed Lady" (I later married one of these). They all captured my imagination, but only one of them captured my heart.

She was "Dahlia" (hermaphrodite). She was big, blonde and beautiful. The gentleman standing outside of Dahlia's tent explained how she was "alive and inside" and standing behind a curtain on a well-lit stage. He told us Dahlia would remove the garments from her body, so in the name of medical science we could see she did indeed possess both male and female genitalia.

Holyshitola! I had never been so excited in my life! I could hardly contain myself. I was going to see a vagina! A real live vagina on a real live woman! Hell yeah, I was excited! I understood Dahlia was sort of like a man, but I didn't care. I was only interested in witnessing her woman parts.

I got in the ticket line, but that's all I got in. I couldn't get inside the tent because I was a "stupid kid." Now, I have been called "stupid" many, many times throughout my life, but this was the first time I had received this moniker, and it hurt.

Feeling rejected and dejected, I wandered hopelessly around the Midway knowing I was never, ever going to see a real live vagina.

While wiping away my tears of disappointment, I happened to glance upwards and there before me, in all of its grandiose glory, stood the Burlesque tent. A palatial canvas pavilion more magnificent, majestic and magical than Cinderella's Castle at Disneyland!

I found myself perfectly positioned to witness the awe-inspiring arrival of five of "the most beautiful women from around the globe," as they seductively strolled out onto an elevated stage. I had never before, nor have I since, witnessed such an impressive sight. Not one, not two, but five wonderful women danced upon the platform and each and every one of them had a vagina!

A nice man walked out onto the stage and invited all of the men to come to a big party the girls were having. He said, "The girls are gonna twitch it and twatch it while you watch it! They've got all the things you like a girl to have and they're gonna shake 'em loose like a bucket of juice! Now guys you've got a choice. You can stand there with your hand in your pocket shaking hands with the unemployed, or you can cum inside. So, step right up gentlemen and get your tickets now!"

It was at this point "The most beautiful women from around the globe" sauntered slowly back into the tent. The nice man announced, "This will be our last and final performance here at the West Virginia State Fair! And even though the law will not allow me to explain the show in front of the women folk, I guarantee it will be the hottest show ever! It will make the old feel young and the young go feeling! It will put a rise in your Levis!"

He informed everyone, "The last and final performance" would soon begin and he'd "only be selling tickets for the next few minutes." He said he would only be selling tickets for "as long as the music plays," but when the music stopped that would be it. No more tickets! He said, "Don't wait, don't hesitate! Now's the time to go if you're going! So, hurry right along now before the music stops! It's show time at the Hoochie Coochie Whirly Girly Revue!"

Having recently discovered erections I was quite excited about the possibility of experiencing one before the long ride home with my parents. However, I knew the nice man was not going to let me into the show because I was just a "stupid kid." Boogers! A tent full of vaginas and I couldn't't get in.

When the music began to play, sheer madness gripped my soul. I didn't know what to do and I panicked. I was crazy with confusion and close to losing my mind, when all of a sudden, like a lightning bolt sent down from heaven, an idea hit me.

I would sneak around to the back of the tent, crawl under it and view the vaginas! It was a brilliant plan! "Stupid Kid?" Ha! I'll show them who's stupid.

"Why hadn't anyone ever thought of this before?" I wondered as I crawled on my belly like a reptile through the thick underbrush. Covered in dirt, fresh cuts and something resembling mayonnaise, I arrived at the rear of the tent. I had made it! I had reached Xanadu!

Peeking underneath the tent, my nostrils quickly filled with the pungent odor of cigarette smoke and vaginas. As I pulled my upper torso into the tent, I was filled with a tremendous sense of accomplishment! Like Alan Shepard, I had managed to go where no man had ever gone before.

In an instant, I was violently ripped out of the tent by a humongous Negro! The black behemoth gripped my arm with such crushing force I was certain he would tear it from my torso and ingest its bloody stump like Shika ate the sailor's.

He carried me squirming and squealing around to the front of the tent where he dropped me to the ground. As I lay there in the dirt with my pants soaked in urine, I heard the music stop and all of my vaginal dreams were destroyed.

Staggering to my feet I ran helter-skelter through the Midway screaming at the top of my lungs. I can't remember my exact words, but I believe they were something along the lines of, "Mommy! Mommy!"

I owe much of my life's happiness to the West Virginia State Fair. For it was there, at the fair, where I discovered gluttony, gambling, and girls.

# NUMBER 63

One Easter Sunday, much like Jesus rose from the dead, I rose from my bed to discover I was experiencing an amazing rebirth. It was my sixty-third birthday and I awoke to the realization I was not only alive but I was living in an extremely healthy and pain-free body.

I became acutely aware of how lucky I was to be so healthy at my age and I asked myself "Why?". What had I done to obtain this high level of health? And I had to say, in all honesty, I hadn't done much. In fact, I believe what I hadn't done had as much of an effect on my health as the things I had done.

Like, I didn't play any team sports when I was in school. I didn't understand the games, didn't enjoy them, and I sucked at all of them, so I simply didn't play. And because of this, I've never suffered any type of sports injury. I've never broken a bone, torn a muscle, or blown out a knee in the pursuit of a ball or another person. I always thought running around chasing things was silly; the only thing I was interested in chasing wasn't even moving. The girls were sitting in the bleachers, not running around in the game.

I didn't get involved in hard alcohol or hard drugs. Now, I'm not saying I've never slammed shots of tequila or packed my sinuses full of cocaine, but these activities were usually on social occasions rather than daily occurrences. I haven't had a drink since March two thousand fifteen; I haven't smoked a joint since lunch.

I also happened to meet and marry a personal trainer and I ate what she ate. So, through no effort on my part, I began eating a clean and healthy diet. My wife prepares nutritious meals and I eat whatever is given to me.

I also happened to meet a psychiatrist at a cocktail party and started seeing her as a patient. I've always suffered from occasional periods of depression. Sometimes it's a mild depression but sometimes it's a deep, dark, debilitating and dangerous depression. I have bi-polar disorder and I will have it for the rest of my life.

There is no cure for this mental illness, but there is treatment. In fact, there are many different treatments for this disorder, and therein lies the problem. The problem is finding which treatment is going to treat the problem without causing even more problems. Discovering which drug or combination of drugs, and in what dosage will allow a person's brain to function properly is a tricky business. So, through no effort on my part I was able to find the doctor who was able to find the drug which works for me.

Because of her I no longer suffer from depression and I now live on the more manic side of life. I have often been accused of being a maniac; today, I'm happy to say, I actually am one. I've never felt so "normal" in my life.

There are many other things which have contributed to my good health, but without a doubt the thing which has contributed the most to my wellbeing is Obamacare.

Now, I know some people are opposed to the Affordable Care Act for political as well as philosophical reasons, and I respect all their various views and opinions on the subject. However, I don't want to spend a great deal of time defending Obamacare, so to those of you who oppose it may I simply say, "Fuck You!"

I was losing my ability to walk and was headed for a wheelchair. I couldn't walk fifty yards without stopping due to the excruciating pain in my back. My feet were going numb to the point where I'd have to stop and grab onto something for fear of falling over. However, because of Obamacare, I was able to have extensive back surgery and now, less than five months later, I'm able to walk, run, jump and ride a bicycle. As a follow-up to my surgery I've had a multitude of tests and thorough physical examinations which have determined I'm in "perfect" health.

So, on Easter morning I awoke to find myself free of depression, free of physical pain and living in an extremely healthy body. WTF? I'd been reborn!

Wow! Reborn! I sure didn't see this one coming. Being reborn can be a little overwhelming at times. It boggles the mind. I mean, getting a "Do-over" on your health is something few men get and I sure as shit didn't want to waste it.

So, as I sat at my computer writing, a reoccurring thought kept crossing my mind. "What do I do with this precious gift which I have been given?" And I thought for quite a while and I decided above all else I was going to protect it. I started protecting my health right then and there by getting out of my chair and stepping away from the machine.

You see, sitting for more than three hours a day is considered to be "excessive sitting" and it will take at least two years off of your lifetime. Sitting is unhealthy. So, as I was sitting there typing, "What do I do with this precious gift which I have been given?" I realized how stupid it was for me to be sitting there typing.

I decided the smart thing for me to do was to get off my ass, get over to the gym, and find out what other people were doing to protect their health.

I walked away from my chair, and I never looked back. I was now on a quest. I was on a quest to find healthfulness and I would begin my journey at the gym.

I decided to start my trip up the Highway to Health by taking a senior fitness class called, oddly enough, "Senior Fitness." The class was scheduled for eleven o'clock in the morning but I showed up an hour early because I've reached an age where I don't always know what time it is, or where I am or even what I'm doing.

As it turned out I was lucky I did arrive early because the health club only lets the first fifty people who show up into the class and I needed a ticket to get in. While standing in line to get my ticket I started talking to a couple of women in front of me and one of those women was a little lady named Pam. Pam is seventy-one years old, petite with short, shiny, silver hair. I told her I'd never taken an exercise class before and she told me: "Relax, It's just a bunch of old people."

As we got our tickets, Pam suggested I go with her to "warm-up" in another class. She said I'd enjoy it because, "The instructor has a nice butt." She took me by the hand and we were on our way.

As soon as we walked into the classroom I took a look at the instructor and thought, "Wow, nice ass!" The room was full of nice asses! Nice shapely asses connected to nice shapely legs which were kicking like crazy. The room was packed with people kicking fast and high like the kicks you see in kung fu movies.

The music was blasting and the instructor was yelling "Kick! Kick! Punch! Kick! Kick! Punch!" Like a manic marine drill instructor with an attractive ass, she was screaming, "Left hook! Left hook! Uppercut! Uppercut! Kick!" and everyone in the room was throwing punches while bobbing and weaving around like Mohammad Ali. Oh! Man! I was in a "Body Combat" class and this shit was intense!

I glanced over at Pam and she wasn't ducking and dodging, but she was shifting her weight from side to side and throwing punches. I don't remember exactly what I was doing, but I know what I wasn't doing. I wasn't staring at the girls.

These women were young, muscular and they moved like lightning. Some of them were wearing boxing gloves and one had lead weights strapped around her ankles. Most of them were dressed in skin tight, low cut, midriff bearing, side boob showing, hip-hugging workout wear. So, I found myself surrounded by a room full of bountiful bouncing boobies and bodacious butts; however, I was too afraid to look at them.

All the walls were covered with mirrors so I could see everybody and everybody could see me. There was no way in hell I wanted one of these battling bitches to catch me staring at her hooters! I mean, although I was fairly confident I could handle Pam, there wasn't another woman in the class who couldn't kick my ass.

Thank God, I was wearing my glasses. I was sure they wouldn't hit an old man in glasses, but to be safe I bobbed and weaved my way closer to the nearest exit.

When the class was over Pam came dancing over and threw a couple of fake stomach punches at my beer gut. She laughed and said, "So, how'd you like it?" I didn't know if she was referring to the class or the instructor's ass, but whatever, I was too out of breath to answer her.

As soon as the Kung-fucken-foo-fighters began to leave the room, the seniors started streaming in for Senior Fitness. Most of them were women, but these women weren't dressed in low cut, midriff baring, skin tight, fashionable workout wear. No, these women were wearing everything from their street clothes to faded T-shirts and old sweatpants. I saw one elderly lady wearing a Jimi Hendrix tank top and another sporting paisley shorts with a Santa sweater.

So, the music started playing and everybody started moving. People were moving left, right, up, down and all around. They were stretching, bending, twisting, kicking, spinning and waving their arms in the air like they just don't care. It was the Hokey Pokey on steroids!

I didn't know what to do, and when I did know what to do, I wasn't doing it right.

I mean, I know this was my first class and all, but this was some simple shit. Easy stuff like raising your arms up over your head. You know, you put your arms up and you take your arms down. Up, down. Up, down. But when their arms were up, mine would be down. When theirs were down, mine were up. It was ridiculous, I couldn't stay with them.

When everybody started moving their arms from side-to-side while stepping back-and-forth I was totally screwed. Not only couldn't I coordinate my movements with the rest of the class, I couldn't even coordinate my upper body's movements with my lower body.

I don't know if it was a matter of conflicting coordination, irregular rhythm, or seeing the reversed images of everyone moving in the mirrors, but I was making my movements late and often in the wrong direction.

I'm well known for moving with amazing rhythm and coordination when I'm horizontal, but I sucked at this vertical stuff.

At one point, we were doing exercises to the James Brown song, "Get on the Good Foot," and I felt like some of the people in the class were rolling their eyes and snickering at me behind my back.

As soon as the class ended Pam came dancing over and said, "Why don't you stay and take the 'Silver Sneakers' class with me? It starts now and its fun!" I told her, "No thanks, I've had enough for one day," and she looked at me with this little puzzled expression on her face and said, "What are you? A pussy or something?"

So, this little seventy-one year-old lady calls me a "pussy" because I don't have the puissance to take two, back to back, one hour exercise classes with her. I would've bitch slapped her if she weren't so adorable.

I told Pam, "My get up and go, got up and went." And she said, "I understand. You don't want to overdo it at your age."

Someone once told me many of these women had out-lived their husbands and they take these classes as a way to socialize and stay fit. And I can understand how they could have outlived their husbands because some of them are probably going to outlive me.

My next stop on the Freeway to Fitness was something called "Zumba Gold." Zumba Gold is a "dance fitness pro-gram for older participants."

If you're not familiar with "Zumba" classes, here's the deal. There was an aerobics instructor in Colombia who fucked up and forgot to bring his aerobics music with him to class. So, he goes out to his car and grabs a couple of old salsa tapes from the glove box. He plays them instead of the traditional aerobics music and makes up a bunch of crazy-ass moves to go with the music.

He bull-shitted his way through an aerobics class and became a billionaire.

Today there are Zumba classes being taught at one hun-dred and forty-thousand locations in over one hundred and eighty different countries. I shit you not! Every week approximately sixteen million people take a Zumba class and today I'm one of them.

Depending upon your age and fitness goals, there are different Zumba classes designed for basically everyone including young children. There's even something called "Kosher Zumba" for Orthodox Jewish women where they've changed the song lyrics to get rid of the nasty stuff.

The Zumba Gold class I was taking uses "easy-to-follow Zumba choreography" designed to help seniors improve their cardiovascular system, flexibility, strength and balance.

The exercises are done to samba, salsa, mambo, reggae and hip-hop music. So, I was a little surprised when the first two women I saw in this dance class were on walkers. Although I must say, seeing them there did boost my self-confidence quite a bit.

You sure as hell could've left your hearing aids at home because the music was blasting, the beat was banging and the seniors were digging it. They were shaking their fannies off. It was like watching your grandparents line dancing to rap music and I was half expecting to see Richard Simmons and Snoop Dogg come prancing into the room at any moment.

We did exercise routines to "The Village People" singing "Macho Man" and Dean Martin singing "Ain't That a Kick in the Head." Everyone went completely bat-shit crazy dancing to Led Zeppelin's "Whole Lotta Love." And, of course we danced to "YMCA" and spelled out all of the letters with our arms. I couldn't figure out how to make the letter "M" but I did make a beautiful "C."

Due to their age and various ailments some of these people were having difficulty moving, but it was obvious to everyone I simply didn't know what the hell I was doing. I was never grooving with the group because by the time I figured out what we were doing everyone had moved on to doing something else. I was always a couple of beats behind and I was happy to be in the back of the class.

I didn't get in the back of the class so people wouldn't see what a spaz I am. I got in the back of the class so I couldn't see myself in the mirror and see what a spaz I am. I don't need to see that mess.

I was, however, keeping a close eye on my fellow class-mates as well as the clock and as we approached the half hour mark I figured this thing must be over soon. I knew I was getting a little winded and I figured thirty minutes was about all these old folks could handle.

And sure enough, the music stopped and everybody be-gan walking away. But they weren't leaving the class, they were walking over to pick up a set of dumbbells for the strength training part of the program. They were all head-ing for a box full of these cute little one, two, three and five-pound dumbbells.

I grabbed a pair of the five-pounders because I figured, "What the hell? I'm younger and stronger than anyone in here." However, I soon regretted my choice because several of the dumbbell exercises were done while balancing on one leg and this was difficult for me to do. My sense of bal-ance sucks and I was wobbling all over the place. Most any-one who knows me will tell you I'm a little unstable.

Now I know using five-pound dumbbells doesn't sound like much, but after waving the suckers around for ten min-utes they felt like concrete blocks. And eventually I had to take a break and put them on the floor.

Dancing around without them was wonderful. I instant-ly felt as light as a feather and I moved with poise and grace. I moved with poise and grace, that is, until I tripped over my own damn dumbbells and BAM! Down I went! I landed pretty hard but no one even reacted to my fall because they were used to seeing my more creative moves.

After class, some seniors came over and said I did "okay." They told me to "hang in there" and assured me it would get easier once I learned the dance moves.

And, speaking of dance moves, the two women using walkers rocked. They sat beside each other in chairs and did as many of the exercises as they physically could for the full hour. They worked out as hard as they could and had as much fun as anyone in the room and I was impressed by their zest and desire to stay fit.

I have to say taking Zumba Gold was well worth my time. I got a good aerobic work-out, stretched every muscle in my body and did some much-needed balance work. Plus, if you've never seen a room full of seniors twerking you're missing out on something extraordinary.

My next adventure on the Road to Robustness was "Spinning®." A Spinning class is a room full of people riding stationary bikes while the pedagogue yells instructions and everyone peddles like they're hamsters on a wheel.

Now, I'm not what you'd call a "morning person" and ordinarily I'd never get up early on a Saturday, but I was pretty excited about taking my first Spin class. So, I hauled my ass out of bed at eight, got on my bicycle and pedaled over to the gym.

When I arrived I wasn't even awake yet, but I said, "I'm doing this!" and marched straight into the classroom. No one else had arrived yet so I was able to get a bike in the back of the room where I wouldn't be so noticeable.

The bikes had fresh towels hanging on the handlebars and I thought this was way cool because ordinarily I'd have to go to the front desk and pick up a towel for myself. Plus, there was a complimentary bottle of water on the bike, which I also thought was a nice touch. Obviously spin class has class.

I immediately started adjusting the bike to fit me. I raised the seat as high as it would go and moved it all the way back to accommodate my long legs. I adjusted the pedal straps so they'd fit over my work boots and I slid the handlebars forward into a comfortable position. It took me quite a bit of time to get the bike adjusted, but never having done it before I thought I did a pretty good job.

I was admiring my work when some cyclists came into the room, pulled the towels off their bikes, climbed on and started warming up. That's when I realized the towel had been placed on this bike by someone so no one else would use it and the bottle of water was theirs. Holy shit! I'd commandeered somebody's bike and completely readjusted it.

I quickly dismounted and moved discreetly to one of the unoccupied bikes in the front of the room. I was careful not to make eye contact with anyone and no one noticed my idiotic behavior.

The music began to play and I was revved up and ready to go. The instructor walked in and told us to start pedaling slowly to warm up. He asked if there were any "first-timers" in the class and I enthusiastically raised my hand. He asked me if I had signed up for the class. He explained how the class was fully booked and all the bikes had been reserved so if I hadn't signed up for the class I would have to leave.

So, I got kicked out of my first class in front of the entire class. Boogers! I registered for next Saturday's class and pedaled my stupid ass back home.

The following Saturday, I signed in with the girl behind the front desk. She checked my name off a list and took a rubber ink stamp and stamped a little black butterfly on my wrist to show I was registered for the class. I hadn't been "stamped" in a long time and it reminded me of my old disco days.

It took me back to a time when the doormen at the discos would put an ink stamp on my wrist when I paid to get into the club. That way if I left the club to go get high or a blow-job or something, they'd know I'd already paid the "cover charge" and they'd let me back in. On a good night, I'd come home with two or three different stamps on my wrist.

So, my little butterfly and I flew into the classroom and I procured a bike in the back. I adjusted its handlebars, seat and pedal straps until everything was perfect. I put my water bottle in the drink holder and I draped my towel over the handlebars so everyone would know this bike was my bike and they'd better keep their damn hands off of it! So, as you can see, I did learn a few things from my first spin class.

I had everything covered. I was thirty minutes early, all set up, and ready to go! And I mean, I was ready to "go." I had consumed three cups of coffee so I'd have plenty of energy for the class and now my digestive system was a gurgling cauldron of coffee-cured-crud. I had more gas than a Chevron station and if I didn't start farting soon there would be some abandoned bikes in the class room later.

The pressure was on. The pressure was on my colon, so I exited the building and headed for the parking lot. I paced back-and-forth in the lot while waving my arm around and yelling into my cell phone as if I were having an argument with someone. No one heard or smelled a thing. Genius!

A friend of mine once told me whenever she takes any type of exercise class she always feels better as soon as she finishes it, but when she takes a spinning class she feels great right away.

The class began and the atmosphere was electric. The music was booming and everyone was fired up and full of life. I was getting a contact high and felt as if I were coming on to some illicit drug. People call this "the energy high" and it was excellent!

I was having an absolute blast, but there was more to this spinning stuff than I realized. As the wheel would spin I'd have to constantly keep adjusting the resistance against it to make the bike harder or easier to peddle depending upon what I was instructed to do. I'd add resistance to "climb hills" and strengthen my legs, or I'd reduce the resistance so I could pedal as fast as possible for several minutes to increase my stamina. Constantly changing the resistance also raised and lowered my heart rate for a great aerobic workout. My goal was to keep pace with the other riders without throwing up or passing out.

I also had to learn how to properly change my riding positions. I'd sit on the seat or stand up on the pedals and change my hand positions on the handlebars according to what the instructor said to do. I didn't understand how it was all supposed to work, but I was learning.

Now, I'm not the sharpest pencil in the box but one thing I did learn rather quickly was jumping up-and-down on those skinny bicycle seats will beat your ball sack black and blue.

I arrived early for my third class and was able to procure the bike I wanted. I adjusted it in no time and when I asked the instructor to check my work she said it was "perfect." Yeah! I got a gold star! I climbed on, strapped my feet on to the pedals, took a sip from my water bottle and I was ready to let-her-rip. Hell yeah, Baby! Let's get it on!

Soon the music was pumping and I was pumping the pedals like a pro. There were fourteen people riding and although I was the oldest, I was still hanging tough. I was off the seat and up on the bars for the hill climbs and I kept my RPMs consistently high throughout the long sprints. I was able to maintain my pace with the other riders and I pedaled nonstop for the entire sixty-minute class.

I did it! I did it! I kicked ass! I was so proud of myself for going the distance and doing it right. It felt awesome and I pumped my fist high into the air and let out a rebel yell in celebration!

And I lost my balance and started falling over. I couldn't put my foot down to catch myself because it was strapped to the pedal so I was in free-fall and slammed into the bike next to mine. And KABLAMY! I crashed a stationary bike! The fucking thing can't even go anywhere and yet I was able to ride it into another bike.

Several people came running to the scene of the collision and pulled me from the wreckage. They helped me to my feet and picked up the bikes. I wasn't hurt and both bikes were okay so nothing was damaged except for my ego. Once again, I'd escaped an accident unscathed and would live to ride another day!

One day as I was trudging up the Trail to Toughness, I decided to start walking on a treadmill. The treadmill has always intimidated me because I'm scared it'll start going really, really, really fast and I'll fall and go shooting right off the back of it. And Zzzooommmm BAM! I sometimes have difficulty separating reality from cartoons.

I see people running on treadmills like the cops are chasing them! I mean, they're flat out flying! They'll get going so fast their legs become a blur and you can hear them gasping for air and they're all sweaty and the belt keeps spinning and spinning and spinning, faster and faster and faster, and it freaks me right the fuck out!

On average, three people die every year in accidents associated with treadmills. It's a damn death machine! I'd rather get on a horse than get on a treadmill and horses scare the bejeezus out of me.

But my friends kept telling me if I wanted to lose weight the treadmill was the fastest way to do it. And although it had been six weeks since I'd had a drink, I still had a "Dicky-do." My beer-belly stuck out further than my dicky-do. And as I've always said, "When a man can no longer see his penis, it's time to put down the fork and step away from the table."

I didn't start out by running on the treadmill. I started out by standing on it. I stood there staring down at the control panel. To me it looked like the dashboard on a space shuttle. It had digital readouts to tell me what my heart rate was, how many calories I was burning, my average speed, my current pace, how far I had traveled, how much time I'd been on the damn thing and how much longer I was going to have to stay on it. This thing made my kitchen blender look like child's play.

There were two big toggle switches located on the cockpit console. The one on the left was used to raise or lower the angle of the revolving belt and the one on the right was used to increase or decrease the rotational speed of the rotating belt. And located right in the center of everything there was a big green button that said, "Quick Start."

Of course, I didn't want a quick start, I wanted a slow start. I wanted a really, really slow start. In fact, I was totally fine with the way things were. I was totally okay with no movement at all. But movement is a prerequisite for any type of exercise so I moved away from the machine.

But I was soon to return. I couldn't give up! If I was going to get six-pack abs before summer I was going to have to overcome my fear of the treadmill. I wasn't crazy about the idea, but I sure as hell didn't want to show up at tanning practice with a spare tire hanging over my Speedos. So, after searching deep within my psyche I discovered a source of strength strong enough to overcome any fear: my enormous ego. Yes, my vanity would carry me to victory! Because at the end of the day, when it's all said and done, it always comes down to my venturesomeness!

Seriously, I'm not making this shit up, you know? "Venturesomeness" is a real word. Google it!

So, I put on my big boy pants, got on the treadmill and pushed the start button like a man. And some digital lights started warning me, "The belt will start in, three, two, one" and BAM! In an instant, the belt started moving real slow! Extremely slow and it wasn't scary at all! Hell, I'd been on escalators that were faster!

Yeah, Baby! I was tread-milling! And after a couple of minutes at level one I kicked it on up to level two and let-her-roll! Yee-ha! My confidence soared and soon I'd accelerated all the way up to level thirty and it felt like when I'm walking. I mean, it felt like I was walking because I was walking. I was walking except I wasn't going anywhere because I was walking on a treadmill, but I was walking like I would've been walking if I was walking on the ground. Like regular old walking, you know what I mean?

So anyway, I was feeling pretty good, not cocky but confident, so I eased it on up to level forty. I started walking kind of fast and it was kind of fun but after thirty minutes I was kind of done. I got to the two-mile marker, but physically I could go no further. Athletes call this, "Hitting the wall," and they push themselves to power through it, but I call it, "Fuck this shit!" and I quit.

Now, I can be as tenacious as a tapeworm but both times I tried to get past the two-mile mark I failed. I was frustrated and ready to give up when I discovered the secret to trekking on a treadmill. I bought a pair of Bluetooth headphones like the old-school ones that cover your ears like earmuffs. Now, I put those suckers on, crank up the blues and walk to the beat. I lose myself in the music and groove right on through the hour. Two miles? No problem.

And I'm not only listening to the music, oh no my friend, I'm playing along with it. I wear heavy leather work boots and when I slam those suckers down it sounds like I'm beating on a big bass drum. It's BAM! BAM! BAM! Baby! Here I come! I dance on the treadmill like Godzilla danced on Tokyo. BAM! BAM! BAM!

Now, I get on one of those whirligigs almost every day. I'm not running, but I'm walking like a bat out of hell and its fun! I'm walking level and I'm walking uphill and I'm walking slow and I'm walking fast and I'm watching TV. That's right, I'm watching TV! I can't hear the TV because I'm blasting the blues, but it's closed-captioned so I can read the TV. I listen to the blues while watching the news! I love the treadmill!

One day while I was Swimming Upstream Toward Strength, I decided I'd take an "Aqua Class." I checked the schedule and there was one immediately following my Spinning® class. So, after beating my balls black and blue on a bicycle seat for an hour I ran over to the swimming pool for my first Aqua class. And although I was fully aware you're not supposed to run around a swimming pool, I ran around the swimming pool and jumped in. I jumped into a cold swimming pool and my testicles shriveled up to the size of peanut M&Ms. My nuts were like little black and blue peanut M&Ms.

So, there I am in the swimming pool and there's thirty of us standing around in chest deep water swishing our arms back and forth in front of us because that's what people do when they stand around in chest deep water.

I was the only man standing in a pool full of women. And these girls were younger than the women I was used to seeing. These nubile nymphs were in their fifties. Most of them were rather large women with big boobies, big booties, and big smiles. These ladies knew each other by name and they were all laughing and joking around with each other like good girlfriends do. This was a happy class and I was happy to be there.

We did some stretching, aerobics and balance work before we started doing strength training with weights. For weight training, we used dumbbells made out of Styrofoam. I shit you not, they were weightless weights. They were Styrofoam weights that floated to the surface. So, to workout, instead of lifting the weights higher into the air, you'd push them deeper down into the water. And like regular dumbbells, the bigger the Styrofoam dumbbell is, the more buoyant it is, thus making it harder to push down, so it's heavier because it floats better or some shit like that.

Many of the exercises were similar to ones I'd done in other senior classes, but because I was doing them in water it was much easier for me to keep my balance. However, because I was moving through water there was more resistance to my movements making it slightly harder to move. And because I was more stable it was easier for me to do the movements correctly and that's why the larger ladies like Aqua Class. The water helps to support their bodyweight so they are more stable and therefore able to do the exercises with better form. Plus, the exercises are not as hard on their ankles and knees.

The class was a gas. I got a good workout and I learned something. I learned it's possible for women to spend an entire hour splashing around in a swimming pool without getting their hair or bifocals wet.

It was pretty cool being the only male in the class. A couple of the females were most helpful, and they encouraged me to come back again soon. Yeah, Baby! I still got it! Chris and thirty women in a swimming pool! Winning!

One day while I was Traveling Down the Turnpike to Wellbeing, I pulled over and parked next to my old friend Pam. She said she was going to take a "Silver Sneakers" class the following day and again she asked me to go with her. I told her I'd never taken a Silver Sneakers class before and again she told me: "Relax, It's just a bunch of old people." She thought I'd enjoy it so I told her I'd go.

So, the next day I'm walking through the gym on my way to meet Pam when I see her on a rowing machine. She's rowing away like crazy, so I asked her how long she'd been warming up. But she wasn't warming up, she'd finished a Zumba class and was cooling off before going to Silver Sneakers with me. I feel so old around this woman.

Pam told me someday she'll be going to a nursing home and when she does she's going to be the hottest babe in there. She said a couple of her girlfriends are in a Home and they're "digging it." I told her she inspired me and I thanked her for talking me into coming to the class with her. She said, "You're easy" and I said, "Everybody knows that."

There were approximately forty people in the class and I was the youngest one there. Most of my fellow classmates looked to be in their seventies or low eighties except for one of the girls who was ninety-two years old. Three of the women there were on walkers, some guy was pushing around one of those three-wheel thingies with the basket on front and another guy was missing his lower right leg and was walking around on a prosthetic leg.

I also noticed there were several people I knew from some of the other senior classes I'd taken and yet when we chose our exercise areas there was no one around me I recognized. It may be my insecurity, but I felt as though those people were keeping a safe distance from me because they'd seen the way I stumble around. But I didn't stumble around all that much because most of the time I was sitting in a chair.

Everyone in the class had a chair, a small rubber ball, a three-foot section of rubber tubing, and a set of dumbbells.

The rubber ball was used for resistance training. We'd squeeze it with our hands, put it under our arm and squeeze it against our body and put it between our thighs and squeeze our thighs together as hard as we could. Squeezing the ball between my thighs reminded me of my old "Thighmaster." You know, the worthless piece of crap Suzanne Somers sells? Mine broke. They're just Japanese junk.

We also used the ball to improve our eye-hand coordination. We'd sit in our chairs and toss it from hand to hand. In your later years your eye-hand coordination decreases, but of course I was the youngest person in the room and the only one who kept leaping out of his chair to chase his ball across the floor. Unless I'm watching porn, I have poor eye-hand coordination.

We used the rubber tubing for strength training. We'd sit in our chairs with the rubber tubing stretched underneath both of our feet and while holding onto the ends, we'd pull our hands up as if we were doing dumbbell curls. We'd hold the tubing out in front of us with one hand and we'd pull back on it with the other hand like we were shooting a bow and arrow. We did numerous exercises using the rubber tubing because the harder you'd pull on it the more resistance your muscles would receive, so everyone was able to work at their own level.

We used the dumbbells for a combination of resistance training and balance work. We'd balance on one leg while raising the dumbbells in front of us, out to our sides and over our heads as a way to increase muscle mass and improve our balance. Maintaining your sense of balance is important as you age to prevent falls and so you can catch yourself if you do start to stumble.

And speaking of "resistance training," have you noticed how I have resisted using the word "dumbbell" as a play on words or in a joking manner? My ability to resist using this word in a funny fashion demonstrates my maturity as a writer.

There was one exercise I enjoyed where we would stand in front of our chairs, slowly sit down on them and slowly stand back up again. Slowly sit down, slowly get up, slowly sit down, slowly get up, thus strengthening the muscles and improving the balance needed to get on and off a toilet. At first it seems a little bit silly, but the reality is when you lose the ability to go to the bathroom without assistance, you lose your independence. And this class was all about helping seniors maintain their independence.

These were functional exercises for independent living. Exercises designed to maintain muscle mass so you can do such things as carry a bag of groceries and put them high up on a shelf. Exercises to improve your flexibility so you can bend over to tie your shoes or pick up a golf ball. This class was about maintaining the strength and agility needed to get in and out of a car or to get down on the floor and play with your grandchildren. This class was about limiting limitations.

It lasted for an hour and we never stopped moving the entire time. I didn't get much in the way of cardio or strength training, but I did get a good full body stretch and I worked on my balance, which is always beneficial for me. And, I must say, I was pleasantly surprised to discover it's much easier for me to coordinate my movements with the rest of the class when we're all sitting in chairs. Baby steps.

But the biggest discovery I made in this class and the others I'd taken is that even though I have been reborn and I'm now living in an extremely healthy and pain-free body, I'm still in pretty bad shape. I'm weak, and I mean I'm weak in physical strength, not only in my ability to resist various vices. Sitting in front of a computer for years drinking Bud Light® was not conducive to a fit physique. But I've stopped drinking and I've started exercising and I'm already in much better shape than I was a few months ago.

I've noticed my overall energy level is way up and so is my endurance. My flexibility and sense of balance has improved somewhat. My mood has definitely improved and my attitude is better. No! Fuck you! I'm serious! My attitude is way better! And, I'm extremely pleased my beer gut has gotten smaller, although I'm a little disappointed my nose is as big as it ever was. But, whatever, this is about improving how I function and feel, not how I look.

Of course, I look great anyway.

# GLORIA

In the 1950s, America's automakers were manufacturing their cars in Detroit, Michigan and it wasn't difficult for them to find workers for their factories. They only had to teach an employee how to perform one or two simple tasks and the worker would stand on the assembly line performing those same simple tasks over and over again throughout the entire day. Throughout the entire week. Throughout the entire year. And some of those workers came from the hills of West Virginia where I grew up.

Some of them were black men from Princeton. Men who would leave their wives and children at home while they traveled north in search of work to support their families. Some of their wives worked as "domestics" and one of those women helped raise me as a young child.

Her name was Gloria Watson and she was big and black. And when I say she was black, I mean she was black. She wasn't dark brown, she was black. And when I say she was big, I mean she was big. She wasn't kinda heavy, she was big. She was big and black and she looked absolutely huge in the eyes of a 7-year-old boy. She was Gloria Watson and I loved her.

Gloria would show up early in the morning and spend the entire day cleaning our home. She would make our beds and wash our dishes, do our laundry and scrub our floors. She worked hard cleaning everything in our house that needed to be cleaned.

Sometimes at the end of a long day my mother would make a pitcher of cocktails and the two of them would sit together on our back patio. They'd drink their toddies, talk and laugh. Occasionally I'd hear Gloria crying. One time I heard my mom.

The three of us loved dancing together. My mother had a collection of 45's and we'd put them on this little-old one speaker record player and boogie around in the kitchen like fools.

Sometimes Gloria would take me out into the backyard where she would put an old quilt down on the grass. I'd take my shirt off and lay face down beside her and she'd scratch my back. When you're a kid there's nothing quite like having your back scratched.

I'd lie in the warm summer sun while Gloria would move her long fingernails rhythmically back and forth across my skin. She'd sing gospel hymns to me and scratch my back for as long as I liked, or until I fell asleep.

I enjoyed the way it made me feel. I felt protected and cared for. I felt loved.

Gloria would make me grilled cheese sandwiches for lunch. She'd put a large cast iron skillet on the stove and melt lots of butter in it. After laying a couple of slices of American cheese between two pieces of Wonder Bread, she'd fry it up in the sizzling hot butter. She'd take a metal spatula and flip the sandwich into the air and catch it, then she'd squash it flat and flip it again.

I'd stand beside Gloria and watch as the fat on the back of her arms would sway back-and-forth as she'd launch my sandwich high up into the air. She'd flip it until it was toasted to a golden brown and slightly burnt around the edges.

No one ever made a cheese sandwich better than Gloria Watson! She'd serve the sandwich to me on a paper plate filled with Lays potato chips and cold pork & beans.

I'd sit in my dad's La-Z-Boy with my lunch on my lap and a cold Coca-Cola by my side. Gloria would stand behind her ironing board with a hot iron by her side.

This was our favorite time of the day. This was one of our most favorite things to do in the whole wide world.

We'd close the curtains in the den so the room would get dark and we'd watch television together. We'd never miss Gloria's favorite TV show, "The Edge of Night."

The Edge of Night was a soap opera much like the soaps of today. Except the show was in black-and-white and always had this creepy organ music playing in the background. Whenever something exciting would happen the creepy organ music would get louder and louder until it reached a fevered pitch.

We'd sit in absolute silence during the show, but whenever a commercial would come on Gloria would jump up from the couch and start ironing. Sometimes she'd disappear into the kitchen only to return moments before the show started again.

The Edge of Night was Gloria's favorite television program, but my favorite show was "Queen for a Day." Queen for a Day was a game show where five women would compete to see which one of them had the most miserable life.

The show's master of ceremonies was Jack Bailey. Jack would introduce each of the women and they would tell him what they'd like to win if they were chosen to be Queen for a Day.

These women weren't asking for luxury items, they were asking for things they desperately needed. Things like beds for their children, home repairs, wheelchairs, dental procedures and stuff like that.

We'd sit motionless and listen to every word as these poor women told stories of their husbands being killed in hunting accidents or their children being crippled by polio or their homes burning down. Stories of broken marriages and broken legs, bankruptcies, tuberculosis, death, disease and horrifying living conditions.

And between each woman's sad story a bevy of beautiful Hollywood models would appear and parade around the studio modeling the latest clothing fashions and jewelry that one lucky woman was going to win.

The curtains would open and the models would bring out brand-new washers and dryers, refrigerators and stoves, dishwashers and storage freezers! And all of these household appliances would be given to the new Queen.

The Queen would also win extravagant prizes such as vacations for her family, along with plenty of money to spend on their fantasy trip.

Yes, one woman would win it all, if she were chosen to be Queen for a Day!

Once the women had finished telling their pathetic tales of woe, the studio audience would be instructed to clap for the one woman they felt deserved to win all the prizes.

Jack would reintroduce the five contestants and as he pointed at each of them the audience would clap. An "Applause Meter" measured the amount of applause each one received and the woman getting the most applause would be crowned "Queen for a Day"!

We'd watch closely to see the disappointment as it appeared on the faces of the desperate women as they realized they were not going to win.

One woman was crowned "Queen for a Day" and a red cape was placed around her shoulders and a crown was placed upon her head. She was presented with a dozen red roses and seated high upon a throne from which she could look down upon the four pathetic losers.

One day as I was sitting in the big chair with my toasted cheese sandwich when Gloria gave me a package. It was a present. She had made a "Queen for a Day" cape for me complete with a crown. I was thrilled! I was jumping around so much Gloria could barely get the outfit on me. But once she did get it on, I was "Queen for a Day"!

Gloria would stand at the bottom of our entrance hall stairs and announce, "Here she is folks! Our Queen for a Day!" And I would walk proudly down the stairs in my cape and crown while holding a bouquet of plastic flowers. As I made my grand entrance I'd smile and wave to the studio audience. Gloria would cheer and clap for me.

Gloria and I always had a good time together, but when I misbehaved she would have none of it. She'd look at me with this stern look on her face and say, "Chris." "Chris" was all she needed to say because when I heard the tone of her voice I knew I was in trouble. I knew I'd been a bad boy and I was going to get a "switching."

Gloria would send me into the woods to get her a "switch." I'd go find a bush and break a young branch off of it and remove all of its leaves. The switch had to be around three feet in length and flexible enough to make a swishing noise when she'd whip it back and forth through the air.

I knew exactly the type of branch Gloria wanted and if she weren't happy with the one I brought her she'd send me right back outside to get her another one.

When I found a switch that suited her, we'd have a discussion regarding what I'd done wrong. Once I had a clear understanding as to why I was being punished, I'd turn around and Gloria would give me some hard whacks across my butt. Thank God she never made me pull my pants down because even with my pants pulled up it hurt like hell!

As soon as my mother would return home Gloria would tell her, "Chris got a switching today." I would have to explain to Mom what I had done wrong. I'd apologize to both of them and promise not to do it again.

Mom never once questioned Gloria's decision to punish me. She knew Gloria loved me as if I were one of her own.

One Saturday morning as I was lying on the floor watching TV, Mom came in and sat down beside me. I thought she was going to watch cartoons, but my mother told me Gloria was dead.

Gloria was dead. I was stunned. I didn't know what to do, but my mother burst into tears and so did I.

Mom had lost one of her closest friends and I had lost one of my mom's.

Gloria's funeral service was held at the Mount Calvary Baptist Church up on High Street. Mom and Dad and I were the only white people in the place but no one cared.

The preacher preached and the choir sang the songs Gloria once sang to me. The people were crying and screaming "Praise the Lord" as they danced around waving their arms in the air.

I could hardly breathe when they lowered Gloria into her grave. People dropped dirt and flowers onto her casket as they walked away.

On our way back to the car Mom took me by the hand and told me Gloria was happy. She said Gloria was with Jesus. I saw Dad give Gloria's husband some money.

None of us said a word on the short drive home, and as soon as we arrived I ran up to my room and cried.

It was the first time I'd thought about death. It was the first time I realized people die.

# 5 HOLES

When I was a young man, I was able to enjoy the glamour and excitement of show business because I was gainfully employed in the motion picture industry. I was the assistant director of a TV series which quite often would film at a location located in one of the seedier sections of Hollywood, which is one of the seedier cities located in the city of Los Angeles.

Above the city of Hollywood there are some mountains and hills known as "Griffith Park," and on the side of one of those mountains there is a hill with a hole in it called "Bronson Caves."

Bronson Caves has been used as a film location since the beginning of time itself. I'd have to write more paragraphs than I'll use in the telling of this entire story to tell you everything there is to know about this hole. So, I'm including a link below where you will find an accurate description of the place and a list of the many TV shows and feature films filmed there.

https://en.wikipedia.org/wiki/Bronson_Canyon

Upon completion of a day's filming at the Caves, I'd often motor down the mountain side to a business venture known as "Jumbo's Clown Room." Jumbo's Clown Room is a strip bar located in a strip mall. Jumbo's is a shit hole.

Now, being a writer, I'd prefer to be using more creative words and phrases to describe the place, but it's just a shit hole. A shitty little bar in a shitty little neighborhood.

I enjoyed going there.

The Clown Room is positioned in an old corner shopping complex which includes an all-night laundromat, a beauty salon and a Mom & Pop grocery selling cigarettes, beer, toilet paper and tampons.

There are no advertisements for dancing girls or neon beer signs flashing in the bar's windows. It has no windows. The place is just one long solid brick wall with an industrial metal door in it and a sign above saying, "Jumbo's Clown Room, Cocktails."

Upon passing through the metal door you walk directly into some disgustingly dirty, heavy cloth curtains which hang from the ceiling. The curtains are a safety device installed to prevent sunlight from entering the barroom and possibly blinding one of its patrons.

Although many find Jumbo's to be a dark, dank dump, full of dangerous desperadoes, I find it to be a magical place full of charismatic characters and cheerful camaraderie.

The interior is best described as "sticky."

It's a dicey bar in a dangerous neighborhood, which caused me some concern because at the time I was driving a new burgundy Porsche and worried someone might steal it.

Back in those days, many people used a device known as a "Steering Wheel Lock." The device was designed to deter would-be thieves. It consisted of two metal rods which were curved in such a way that the end of one of the rods wrapped around the automobile's steering wheel, while the end of the other rod wrapped around the automobile's brake pedal. The straight end of the brake pedal rod would slide inside the straight, hollow end of the steering wheel rod. The two rods were then pushed together and secured in place with a lock and key. Once installed, the device prevented car thieves from being able to turn the steering wheel or use the car's brakes. Genius!

I always put my steering wheel lock on the car before entering the speakeasy. By installing the device, I was able to relax in the road house, confident in the knowledge my car was secure and no one could steal it.

Upon entering the beer garden cabaret one day, I procured a seat at the bar. The anorexic barmaid was busy catering to the pub's clientele of derelicts, drifters, dopers and insurance salesmen. I flagged her down and ordered a Heineken. I always ordered Heineken because the majority of the other patrons preferred Budweiser. I felt drinking Heineken lent me a certain air of worldly sophistication.

As she delivered my beer, she also placed a bag of Ruffles and a can of bean dip on the bar. After unceremoniously ripping the tin lid from the bean dip, she declared it was "Happy Hour!" and all drinks were now half price. Damn!

I'd missed it by a matter of seconds and had to pay full price!

While heading towards the men's room to drain the lizard, I happened to spy Dorene putting coins into the jukebox. I strolled over, gave her a squeeze and after we exchanged pleasantries, I offered to buy her a drink.

She sat on the barstool next to mine and seductively wrapped her moist lips deep down around the business end of a bottle of Bud. I asked her if she was a hooker or an undercover cop or something and she assured me she was safe.

I kept a close eye on her in the mirror behind the bar. I wanted to see how the two of us looked sitting together. In all honesty, I'd have to say I was looking great! Image is everything in Hollywood.

We joked and laughed like old friends while hammering beers and discussing the geopolitical situation of the day. Dorene wasn't like the other girly girls. She was coherent.

Dorene had god-given talent and I was mesmerized when watching her dance. She had protrusions on her chest which had the power to attract men's eyes. I'd watch her bountiful breasts spinning around and around the stripper pole as if moving in slow motion. The tassels on her pasties fluttering back softly in the breeze.

I like big boobies, and I can't deny it!

Now, I'm not sure how, but she persuaded me to take her to my place. So, we stepped out of heaven and into the hellish heat of the smog-filled city. You could taste the air and it burned your throat when you breathed.

The hotness sucked the moisture from our skin as we strode hand in hand towards my two-seater.

Dorene was quite impressed by my ride, as she should be, and I was smiling as I slid into my car, knowing we would soon be sliding into my bed and I would soon be sliding into her. Yes, I was in a pretty good mood.

I was in a pretty good mood, that is, until I started to unlock the steering wheel and discovered the key had broken off my key ring.

OMG! It was gone!

After frantically searching in my pockets, in the car and in the parking lot, I concluded it was in the Clown Room. Reluctantly we reentered the joint to find the key to happiness. We looked everywhere from our barstools to the bathrooms. Searching the floor, our heads bobbing up and down like chickens pecking the ground, looking for food.

A couple of the girly girls walked over with a flashlight to assist us in our search. A couple of the manly men walked over to assist the girly girls. Even the dancing lingerie model abandoned her pole mid dance and began looking for the wayward key.

While spending more and more time looking for the key, I started looking more and more at my girl and she started looking less and less like the girl I thought I was looking at.

When out of nowhere this young girl walks up and wants to know what's going on. She wasn't a girly girl, she was a local girl stopping by for a cold one. She was a girl in the girly bar but not one of the girly girls, just a regular ol' girl who happened to be drinking in the girly bar. I began telling her my tale of woe when out of nowhere Dorene walks up and wants to know what's going on.

Dorene wasn't pleased I was conversing with the young lady and suggested perhaps my newfound friend should "Fuck off!" The girl walked away, and I told Dorene I felt her behavior was somewhat rude and uncalled for. Dorene suggested I should "Fuck off!"

Before you know it, we're shouting dirty words at each other and in the heat of the moment, I made a mistake and used the "C" word. I had a steady girlfriend, so I knew you never, never, ever, ever use the "C" word in such circumstances. But somehow it slipped past my lips and Dorene went absolutely postal on my ass! She was on me like white on rice!

She was screaming and cussing and slapping and kicking me, so of course some members of the military raced to her defense and vigorously pummeled me with their fists. The courageous commandos drug me across the saloon floor, through the disgustingly dirty curtains, through the metal door and threw me on to the hot pavement of the parking lot!

Okay, so that's not exactly how it happened. I made up all that shit about the fight and stuff to make the narrative more exciting. I lied because, let's face it, looking for a car key is not great subject matter for a story. I'm sorry. I knew I shouldn't have done it, but I did. I'm sorry.

The truth is, all Dorene did was call me some dirty words and tell me to leave. So, I walked through the disgustingly dirty curtains and out the metal door much like I'd walk out the door any other time I was walking out the door. I casually walked out the door and into the bright California sun.

And there in the bright California sun sat my car. Still parked in the parking lot. No one had stolen it. I couldn't take it, and I owned it!

I'm suffocating in the extreme heat and pissed off! I'm hopping around praying, ranting and raving! I'm stomping around in little circles not knowing what to do when out of nowhere this young boy rides up on a bicycle and wants to know what's going on.

Now I'm not sure how, but he persuaded me to give him twenty dollars. He told me he was going to ride his bicycle to a hardware store and purchase a hacksaw with which to cut the lock off of my car. So, I gave him the money and down the road he rode.

I sat on the hood of someone's car and waited, and waited, and waited. I waited and waited. And then I waited and I waited and guess what?

He came back! He came back with a hacksaw and a set of five hacksaw blades, because, as he explained, "When you're cutting through steel with a cheap-ass-hacksaw the blades tend to break."

The young lad explained how it was difficult and time-consuming to saw through the steering wheel lock, but it was quick and easy to saw through the steering wheel itself. He said it was a snap to cut through the steering wheel and remove the lock. He said he could do it in under three minutes!

I said, "Thanks, but no thanks!" and proceeded to explain how this was a costly car manufactured in Germany, not a Ford Fiesta. I told him to keep the change and down the road he rode.

I got in the driver's seat and proceeded sawing on the wheel lock. I was sawing, sawing, sawing and sawing and it was not going well. In fact, it wasn't going at all, and after working in the hellish heat for over half-an-hour the tool slipped and I cut a gash in my left hand. This was bloody bullshit! When the third blade snapped, I snapped!

Realizing there were only two blades left, I knew that if I didn't take the kid's advice I could be sitting in this parking lot for the rest of my natural life.

I mean, he did seem to speak from experience, and although I wasn't too keen on the idea of cutting through the steering wheel of my new Porsche, I proceeded to take the cheap-ass-hacksaw and slice through the soft, supple leather which was meticulously sewn around it.

I hacked through the steel of the wheel in less than three minutes!

Ripping the wheel lock from the wheel, I screamed, "Fuck off!" and threw the piece of shit into the parking lot! I stepped on the gas and down the road I rode. My hand hanging out of the window, so as not to get more blood on the leather interior.

# WALK LIKE A MAN

When I was a young child I was unable to walk. Physically I was capable of walking, but I couldn't do it. I either lacked the necessary motor skills or the desire or something, but whatever it was, I could not walk.

All of my contemporaries could walk. Many of my mother's friends had children my age who were walking all over the place. Although I excelled at sitting around, rolling around and crawling around, I did not walk around. I have always been an embarrassment to my family and I believe this lifelong pattern of disappointment started with my inability to walk.

If I was not going to stand up and walk like a man on my own, someone was going to have to teach me how to walk. My Granddaddy Eddins took on this tremendous task because he was tired of seeing his grandson scooting and thrashing around on the floor like a retard.

Now today, no caring adult would ever refer to a young child exhibiting an inability to develop basic skills as a "retard," but back in the fifties it was a common term and in this particular instance it certainly applied to me.

Granddaddy Eddins loved me as only a grandfather can love a child. It was his ingenuity, patience and determination which got me up off my knees and raised my diapered ass into the air.

My Granddaddy would extend his index finger to me over and over again. He'd tease me with his finger by keeping it just a teeny-weeny bit out of my reach. I'd make a move for the finger and the finger would move. It was a game he would play with me.

We'd play "Catch The Finger" and whenever I was quick enough to catch his finger I would not let go. If I caught the finger, I'd hold on as tight as I could and Granddaddy would pull me around on the floor. He could move his finger in this direction or that direction, up or down and all around, but I would not let go. Eventually he could raise his finger up into the air and I would hold on, stand up and go wherever his digit directed. Hallelujah! I was walking.

Yes, I was walking. However, I was only walking when the finger was around. If I wasn't with the finger, I wasn't going anywhere on my feet. I've never been one to exhibit a great deal of self-confidence and I believe my dependence on family and friends first developed with my reliance on his finger.

I'd hold onto my grandfather's finger and the two of us would stroll around the house. I could travel near and far with the finger, but one day the finger abandoned me.

Granddaddy replaced his finger with a short section of string. He'd hold onto one end of the string and I'd hold onto the other and off we'd go. From the bathroom to the bedroom, kitchen to the den, it didn't matter where he would go I'd hold on to the string and walk along with him.

One day he took me out into the front yard to demonstrate my newfound talent to his friends. Granddaddy would hold his end of the string and I'd hold mine, and he would parade me around the yard as if I were a show horse.

Look at him go! Look at him go! Everyone was so proud of me until the moment my grandfather would let go of the string. If the string dropped, I dropped. Whenever the string hit the ground so would my butt.

Eventually, I did learn to walk on my own. However, walking was never my forte. I was also not particularly good at running, jumping, skipping or hopping.

For many years I walked on my toes. I didn't lower my heel to the ground and roll my foot forward and up on to my toes as I walked. No, I walked "tippy toed" all the time. By springing from foot to foot I'd bounce along, which added a certain pep to my step.

Toe walking is a common occurrence among young toddlers as they learn to walk, especially during their first and second years of life. And although the tendency often goes away by the age of three, in some kids it may last a little longer. In my case it lasted well into my fifties.

I was unaware of my bouncy behavior until I became a cadet at Fork Union Military Academy. In military school, they teach the cadets to march. We would march everywhere. We'd march to class. We'd march to meals. We'd march to bed. We would march in military parades where we would march around demonstrating our ability to march.

Summer was a special time at Fork Union. Every Sunday, after chapel services, the cadet corps would suit up in our full-dress summer uniforms and present ourselves in company formations for inspection. We would march out onto the grass-covered parade grounds before a large stadium filled with parents, guests and military dignitaries. It was a big deal.

We cadets dressed in gray West Point uniforms, white pants, white gloves and white hats while carrying a rifle. The officers dressed in gray West Point uniforms, white pants, white gloves and black hats, while sporting a wide red sash around their waist and carrying a saber.

The military band would play as the entire cadet corps marched in perfect lock step out onto the parade grounds. We would stand at attention in our company formations with our platoon flags waving in the breeze and our rifles held steady at our sides.

Various dignitaries would give speeches, the band would start to play and we'd parade before the reviewing stand, saluting as we marched past. I must say it was quite an impressive sight when observed from the grandstands.

Later in the week we'd watch a film of the parade to see how we might improve our performance. Viewing the film, one would witness an endless sea of white hats flowing in unison across the parade grounds. Except for the one single hat which was bobbing up and down to its own unique rhythm. My hat, demonstrating to myself and all others the unique way in which I moved upon this earth.

I was also blessed at birth with a condition known as "genu valgum," commonly known as, "knock-kneed." It's a condition in which the knees angle in and touch one another when the legs are straightened. It's a normal condition in children between the ages of two and five years of age and will naturally resolve itself as the child grows older. Personally, I didn't naturally resolve myself of this condition until "never."

Now, I am not looking for sympathy. Being knock-kneed has never been much of a problem for me. My problems have been mostly mental or emotional in nature. However, as anyone who has ever witnessed my snow skiing skills will tell you, I have a problem.

Snow skiing requires the ability to keep one's skis pointed in the same direction and parallel to each other. This isn't hard for me to do, but it's hard on my knees when I do it. Because if my feet are parallel, my knees are pointed inward and touching. When I ski moguls, my knees start banging each other like two teenagers on ecstasy.

Water skiing is much the same, albeit a bit more embarrassing. When snow skiing, my legs are concealed inside padded ski pants, whereas when water skiing my lanky legs are exposed for all to see. I not only have knock knees, I also have knobby knees. I have big knobby knock knees on skinny scrawny legs. Chicks dig it!

In my prepubescent years my Father often referred to me as "Bird Legs." If I happened to walk by while wearing a pair of shorts my Dad would call out, "Bird Legs! Tweet! Tweet!" I can tell you, it was a real confidence builder for a young kid.

The shape of my legs also shaped my athletic career. As a youngster, my legs may have been thin, but they were long and I could run like the wind. I could outrun my Mother, Grandmother, maid, and babysitter.

Most of my early running was done around swimming pools. I ran for the sheer joy and exhilaration of running. I loved to run. I loved to run, that is, unless someone was forcing me to run.

I despised running in my physical education class. Our PE teacher, who always stood in one place, would make us run laps around the gym. Why? What was the point of running around and around only to end up where you started? I thought this was stupid and hated doing it. However, I did discover that if I ran at the end of the line I didn't have to run as fast or for as long as the other kids.

Although today I gladly pay seventy-eight dollars a month to go to the gym, when I was young I thought it sucked and would use any excuse to get out of going.

I was so jealous of the girls because they could get out of going to PE class simply by having their period. Every month they got a "Get out of jail free card" for riding the cotton canoe. PE sucked; so, no matter how horribly sick I would become, I was delighted to catch any illness, disease or disorder which was currently infecting the children at school.

Being too sick to go to school was one of life's finest pleasures. I relished it. I got to stay home and lie around on the couch while the other kids were in school, sitting at their desks. I was watching cartoons in the den while those losers were running around in the gym. Yes, I loved being confined to the couch because my Mother was there to cater to my every whim.

My Mom made "being under the weather" wonderful. I'd lounge in my jammies, propped up on fluffy pillows while wrapped in a comfy comforter for warmth. I'd have a fully stocked TV tray containing crackers, tomato soup, buttered grilled cheese sandwiches, and a large glass of 7Up on the rocks. Mom always gave me saltine crackers and 7Up because she thought they would "settle" my stomach and prevent me from throwing up.

However, puking wasn't a problem. Mother would lay a couple of old beach towels beside the couch so if I did become nauseous I could lean over and vomit on the floor. Genius.

So, I was always delighted to catch any illness and illness was the only thing I could catch. You see, when I was around nine years of age my Mother took me out into our front yard to play a game of "catch." She was going to teach me how to catch a baseball while wearing a baseball glove.

It was a gorgeous sunny summer day. Our lawn was recently mowed and the mountain air was filled with the sweet smell of freshly cut grass. We were excited, ready and eager to play. This was going to be fun!

We took our positions. Mom was the pitcher and I was the catcher. And, there's the windup! And, there's the pitch! And, BAM! Mom nailed me right in the fucking face! Blood shot out of both nostrils and tears flowed out of both eyes. The game was called on account of hysterics.

Now whenever I detect any type of projectile moving in my direction I immediately try to dodge it. My knee-jerk reaction is to duck, avoid, evade, recoil, or run for cover. I can't catch a baseball, football, basketball, tennis ball, or golf ball worth a shit. Toss me the car keys and watch me pick them up off the ground.

Of course, I know what you are thinking. You're thinking I must have been a brilliant Dodge Ball player. And you're right. In PE class I had this whole Dodge Ball thing figured out. As soon as the opposing team possessed the ball, I'd run toward them, stop, and stand still. I'd get hit with the ball and go sit down. I would kick back and relax while watching the other kids running around like fools. Genius.

Although I did play various sports as a kid I can say without hesitation or trepidation, I sucked at all of them. I always knew I sucked at all of them, but I didn't care because I always thought they all sucked.

I've always found team sports to be boring. I've never had any interest whatsoever in being a part of "the team." Some would call me a "loner;" however, I enjoy my own company and I'm easily amused. I excel at doing nothing and I've made "lounging" into an art form. You cannot get a deep, dark, even tan like mine while moving around and doing stuff.

I do have a couple of stories about my short athletic career and since this is a short story I will include them here.

Basketball: It's the fourth quarter and the score is tied. Somehow, I get possession of the ball and no one is guarding me. I turn. I dribble. I shoot. I score! The crowd goes wild! My entire team leaps to their feet! I can't believe it! I did it! I scored! Unfortunately, it was the wrong basket and I put the opposing team up by two.

Golf: I loved racing around the course in the carts, but golf was way too slow and tedious for me. I have no interest in standing around and waiting while other people do stuff.

Track: Fuck that shit! I've already described my detestation for running around in circles.

Football: One night as my family was sitting around the dinner table, my Father inquired as to how my little league football practice was going. I was delighted he asked because I knew he loved the game and how much he wanted to see his son succeed.

I was showing him how I'd learned to fake-out my opponent. "This is how you do it Dad. You fake left and you move right!" And BAM! I ran straight into the back of a chair, driving my upper teeth through my lower lip. I fell back onto the floor, crying and bleeding profusely.

Dad scooped me up into his arms and raced out our back door. We were headed for Doctor Joe's. Doctor Joe McCary was a long-time family friend and he lived nearby.

I'll never forget the look of fear in my Father's eyes as he ran through the cold, moonlit night cradling me in his arms as if I were a baby. Faster and faster he ran until we were moments away from reaching Dr. McCary's back porch. And BAM! My Father's neck connected with Mrs. McCary's clothesline. In an instant, he had hung himself and his legs flew out from beneath him. We were both slammed to the ground. Dad was coughing and bleeding. I was bleeding and screaming. Dr. and Mrs. McCary came rushing to our rescue. They stitched us up and cleaned us up and soon my Father and I were walking hand in hand back to our home.

Baseball: Please reread the previous paragraphs relating to my Mother and me playing catch.

For the next couple of decades my walking abilities were much like anyone else's. I was able to move from point "A" to point "B" without any problem. My feet and legs were more than capable of carrying my ass around.

And may I take a few moments here to point out what a fine ass it is. Next to my rugged good looks and pleasant personality, my small, perfectly proportioned, round ass is one of my strongest attributes. Women love it and throughout my life I've been able to slip my booty into a pair of tight jeans and let the good times roll. However, I shall not get sidetracked at this time by digressing into describing the many attractive attributes of my ass. This in itself is another story, which at this time is better left behind.

Yes, other than the occasional "trip" down the stairs or "slip" in a bar's bathroom, I was pretty good at perambulation. However, when I was around fifty-four years old I had an accident that may have caused me damage. I was ripping down Topanga Canyon Boulevard at an excessive rate of speed when I collided with a collie. I was on my skateboard and the damn dog ran right out in front of me.

First I hit the dog, then I hit the sidewalk. The dog was fine, but I was fucked. I was out like a light. I don't know how long I was unconscious, but I woke up dazed and confused. And I mean much more dazed and confused than usual.

When I was fifty-eight, I suffered another accident while sitting at a traffic light one night. I happened to glance into my rearview mirror when "Oh fu--" a speeding BMW slammed into me. I didn't even have time to get the "ck" out. The car hit me so hard it knocked me across four lanes of traffic and into a light pole.

How I got through the intersection without being broadsided by another car is nothing short of a miracle. Luckily, I was able to climb out of the mangled machine and wobble away.

I walked away from the wreck, but the wreck followed me. I soon started to experience slight pains shooting down the backs of my legs. This wouldn't happen often, and when it did it was only an annoyance.

There are many things I enjoy doing in this life, but the thing I enjoy the most is cuddling. Nothing compared to being in bed and snuggling with my wife. The magic of lying in a comfy cozy cocoon while wrapped around her beautiful bare body was indescribable.

Every morning Christine and I enjoyed breakfast in bed. We set the alarm an hour early and when it went off my wife prepared a couple of delectably delicious protein shakes. We would drink a wholesome breakfast while lying in bed, wrapped around each other and drift off to sleep until it was time for us to get up and start our day.

I began noticing numbness in my right leg, much like the tingling feeling you get when your arm or leg goes "to sleep" from lack of blood circulation. I liked to sleep with my right leg positioned between Christine's thighs. Therefore, we thought the numbness could possibly be caused by this sleeping position. Maybe my numbness was nothing more than a "cuddle injury."

So, to correct the problem we began mixing things up. One night I'd sleep on the left side of our bed and the following night on the right. With much determination and some difficulty, I was able to prevent my right thigh from sliding in between hers and, lo and behold, the numbness soon subsided. We were correct, the numbness was a "cuddle injury."

Except it wasn't a "cuddle injury." My feet began to go numb to the point where I was no longer able to feel them. It felt as if I had no feet at all and was walking on my ankles. It was like standing on sticks.

Whenever this would occur, I'd be forced to stop walking for fear of losing my balance and falling over. Although I was concerned, this was only an occasional annoyance, which was easy to deal with. All I'd have to do was stop for a moment, lean against something and stretch out my calf muscles.

You see, because of my constant toe-walking my calves were overworked and would therefore become as hard as a rock. Perhaps this was restricting the blood flow to my feet and causing the numbness.

Who knew, but whatever it was, it wasn't much of a problem. Like I said, I'd stop, stretch my calves and be on my merry way.

Christine was convinced my toe-walking, forward head, rounded shoulders and overall piss poor posture were contributing to my problems. Not only is my wife a personal trainer and lifestyle coach, she is also a certified corrective exercise specialist.

She began working with me to correct my postural problems. She taught me how to walk by rolling forward from the heel of my foot up onto the ball of my foot while maintaining my spine in a neutral position, core fully engaged, tailbone slightly tucked under with my shoulder blades relaxed, back and down.

She instructed me in a program of strength training, flexibility, and balance work. Like my Granddaddy Eddins had once done before her, Christine was now teaching me how to walk.

Even though I was able to achieve much improvement in my overall posture, the level of pain I was experiencing had progressed to the point where I was unable able to walk fifty yards without having to stop, rest and stretch.

This was no longer an occasional annoyance; now I was scared. I was scared because I knew I was losing my ability to walk. I couldn't afford medical care and I didn't know what I was going to do. But then something wonderful happened.

I was riding my motorcycle through Grimes Canyon, on a curvy road carved into the side of an extremely steep mountain. I was traveling up the two-lane road with the mountainside to my right and a sheer drop off to my left. I approached a tight right-hand turn at excessive speed and lost control of the motorcycle.

Shooting cross the center line, I was but a nanosecond from jettisoning out over a cliff. There wasn't a guard rail to stop me, only a small sandy berm, which would have launched me high out over the hillside where I'm certain I'd have fallen to my death. But I got lucky. I slammed head-on into an oncoming automobile.

Crashing into the car stopped my forward motion and saved my life. The abrupt impact threw me into the air. The bike hit with so much force it cut the cylinder heads off of its motor and tore the right front wheel off of the car. If my right leg had not been up in the air it would have been severed.

I was thrown into the car's windshield where the shattering safety glass somewhat cushioned the blow. Bouncing off the moving automobile, I landed on the edge of the cliff with the motorcycle tumbling down upon me. The bike pinned me to the ground and once again I was prevented from going over the edge of the cliff.

Looking around I realized I was still alive. Looking down I realized I still had my legs. Staggering to my feet, I realized I could still walk and started down the road toward the car.

Approaching the automobile, I could see two children's car seats through its back window and my heart stopped with the realization of what I had done. As I reached the car, I was able to see the car seats were empty and the driver was getting out.

We grabbed onto one another and started saying, "Are you okay? Are you okay?" I was so relieved to hear her say, "Yes."

The accident scene was soon swarming with police, firefighters, and paramedics and each and every one of them was wonderful. The Highway Patrol officer was more than helpful. The firemen and paramedics who examined me were professional, thoughtful, and thorough.

I cannot say enough about the woman whose car I hit. Not only did she handle the situation without any drama or incriminations, she saved my life. God knows what would've happened had she not been there on that fateful day.

Upon being examined, it was determined my blood pressure was normal given the circumstances and there was no sign of a concussion or broken bones.

"How do you know I don't have any broken bones?" I asked. To which the paramedic replied, "Because you'd be in extreme pain. Now let's get you into the ambulance and to the hospital where we can check you out." "No thanks," I said. "I'm not going to the hospital, I'm going home. You said I don't have any broken bones. If I start pissing or shitting blood, I'll go to the emergency room." I put my bruised and bleeding body onto the back of a friend's motorcycle and we rode home.

For the next couple of weeks I lay in bed sleeping, surfing porn, and licking my wounds. With the assistance of a steady stream of Bud Light and whatever pain pills my friends were willing to donate to my cause, I was able to make a miraculous recovery.

Like I said, "I got lucky." Not only had I escaped the accident with my life, but I had escaped it without lawyers. I had suffered neither excessive injuries nor excessive expenses.

The insurance I had at the time was the basic auto insurance required by the state of California. If I had been sued by the woman I hit or if either one of us had incurred medical expenses, I could have lost my home and all I'd ever worked for. The thought of losing everything was as terrifying as the accident itself.

This was a wakeup call I had to answer. I knew I could no longer postpone purchasing health insurance. I'd always had private insurance but being self-employed, a/k/a "unemployed," the premiums had reached the point where I could no longer afford them.

After an exhaustive search for a suitable insurer, I was unable to find one which met my insurance needs. They all wanted money and I wanted benefits; therefore, we could not agree on an agreeable agreement.

I became so frustrated and discouraged I said, "To hell with it!" and stopped looking. I had given up all hope until one evening I was fortunate enough to be watching FOX News when Sean Hannity and Sarah Palin were discussing the many benefits of the Affordable Care Act.

They said it was a progressive program which was proving to be so popular the governmental computer programs were overwhelmed by the sheer number of people trying to purchase policies. In fact, Sean said people were willing to wait for hours to apply! This certainly sounded good to me.

Now, although it was the "Affordable Care Act," Sarah and Sean kept calling it "Obamacare" because they said our President was responsible for the program and I guess they wanted to make sure he got full credit for the good thing he had done.

Christine and I drove over to the Department of Public Social Services building to see what this Obamacare stuff was all about. When we walked into the place it was packed. I mean it was shoulder to shoulder, ass to ass, wall to wall people. We had brought our iPads along with us in anticipation of being there for a while, but the sheer size of the crowd was ridiculous.

We muscled our way to the reception desk and explained how we were interested in learning about Obamacare. Without even looking up, the man behind the counter pointed towards a door and said, "Its down that hallway, last door on your right."

Upon following his directions, we walked to a small office consisting of a desk and four chairs. There was no one waiting in the hall and no one sitting in the chairs. A lady was seated behind the desk and we sat down in the chairs.

Christine and I explained our situation to the lady. She pulled our tax records up on her computer, looked a few things up in a thick book, handed us a couple of forms and showed us where to sign. And BAM! We were insured. No wait, no worries.

During my initial physical exam, I explained in detail my difficulty walking and the painful symptoms I was experiencing. The first question the doctor asked me was "How much alcohol do you drink?" WTF? I sure didn't see this one coming. This was the first time I'd ever considered alcohol could somehow be the cause of my problems.

I knew the doctor needed this information in order to make the correct diagnosis so of course I lied. "Oh, I'd say one or two beers a day." To which he replied, "Uh-huh."

After denying my request for Viagra, he wrote me a prescription for 800 mg ibuprofen. X-rays were ordered and I was given an appointment to see an orthopedic specialist.

As I sat waiting in the specialist's examination room with my x-rays in hand, I started reading the various diplomas hanging on the wall. This doctor held several different degrees. One was from the University of Cairo and two were from Harvard University. He specialized in orthopedic and spinal surgery as well brain surgery and I was grateful to be sitting in his office.

Upon entering the exam room, he introduced himself, took a quick glance at my x-rays and exclaimed, "Wow! Man!

Do you have a messed up back!" This was not quite the level of professionalism I expected from a Harvard grad.

He proceeded to explain how I was suffering from "degenerative anterolistehesis of L-4 and L-5, severe L-4 L-5 canal stenosis, severe L-4 L-5 foraminal narrowing with impingement of the existing right L-4 nerve root, moderate to severe L-3 L-4 canal stenosis, left L-3 L-4 moderate to severe foraminal narrowing and L-1 L-2 mild canal stenosis." Or, in layman's terms, "A messed up back."

He told me that in most cases like mine the first thing doctors will do is to try different types of physical therapy. If the therapy doesn't relieve the pain they will prescribe various pain killers or cortisone shots. He said there were many ways to approach my problem, however they would only be a waste of time and money. I needed surgery and I needed it now because I had "A messed up back."

I signed a couple of papers, an MRI was ordered and a tentative surgery date was set pending approval from my insurance company. I was stunned. I couldn't believe it. I was going to have surgery to fix my back!

A week or two later, I received a call telling me to get ready to pack my bags because I'd soon be returning to New Zealand for another year of work on the TV show "Power Rangers." This was great news. I was going back to do what I do best, "Kung-fu fightin and blowin things up reel good." This was awesome!

Except it wasn't awesome. I was scheduled to return to New Zealand six weeks before I was scheduled to have my surgery.

Well, this sucked because I was now going to have to postpone the surgery. I had no choice. I'd been with the show ever since we filmed the first episode. I'd been doing this for over eleven years and I loved my job. The director of photography and I had filmed 587 episodes together and I wasn't going to let him down. Plus, Christine and I needed the money. The surgery would have to wait.

Except the surgery couldn't wait. When I explained my situation to the doctor, he explained my situation to me.

He explained how the nerves in my spine could possibly be pinched to the point where I'd be unable to walk. There was also the possibility some of my internal organs would cease to function and I could die.

He couldn't predict how long it might be before these things could happen, or even if they would happen, but there was a distinct possibility they might happen.

I was freaking out! I needed the surgery, but I also needed the money. I wanted to return to New Zealand to be with my friends, but I was scared of what might happen if I were to go.

Perhaps the surgery could be scheduled for when I came home for Christmas? Perhaps Power Rangers could start the season without me and after the surgery I could fly down and join them?

I was talking to people in Los Angeles, Japan, New Zealand and Spain trying to work things out, but it wasn't working. This continued for weeks and the indecision was tearing me up. I was an emotional wreck and unable to sleep. I was so worried and I didn't know what to do. But then something wonderful happened.

I lost my job. The production company replaced some people with some people who replaced me. I was crushed. In an instant one of the greatest pleasures of my life was taken from me. I cannot put into words what a devastating experience this was. Not only had I lost my job, but in many ways, I had lost my purpose in life.

The date of my anticipated departure passed and the date of my surgery arrived. I walked into the hospital with nothing more than the clothes on my "messed up back."

Checking in was much like checking into the Hilton. I was greeted with a cheery, "Good morning, sir. May I help you?" "Yes, my name is Joseph Auer and I'm here for surgery," I replied. "Yes, sir," he said, "have a seat in the lobby and someone will be with you soon. Enjoy your day."

I was escorted into a room where I was prepped for surgery. I gave up my clothes and was given a gown. I gave up my blood and was given a bracelet. The admitting nurse quizzed me with some fairly easy multiple-choice questions before two orderlies laid me onto a gurney and started pushing me through the corridors of the hospital.

As I lay there staring up at the ceiling, I was struck by two realizations. First, I realized the POV camera angle they always use in television shows when someone is being pushed through a hospital hallway is accurate. You know the one where you see the ceiling moving with light fixtures passing by? Well, that's what it looks like.

I also realized I was not in the least bit nervous. I knew all surgeries involved a certain amount of risk, but I felt no fear. I was prepared for whatever fate might lay before me.

I had kissed my wife goodbye and told her no matter what might happen she had made my life worth living and I would love her for all of eternity. I had thanked my father for giving me life and bringing me into this world. I'd told my sister how much I loved her. I'd cleaned my computer's hard drive of any incriminating evidence or embarrassing items in case I'd happen to die. Yes, I was relaxed and ready.

But upon hearing the elevator doors closing behind me my heart rate quickened and my mind filled with a thousand unanswered questions. "Why wasn't there a word which rhymed with Orange? Who killed JonBenet Ramsey? Why didn't Farrah Fawcett divorce Ryan O'Neal when she had the chance? If Eric Clapton shot the sheriff, who shot the deputy?" Perhaps I may never know.

Arriving in the operating room, I was informed my surgeon had called to say he was stuck in traffic but would be arriving soon. The assisting surgeon, nursing staff and I passed the time by comparing our various tattoos and piercings.

Bob Marley was playing over the sound system. I shit you not, they were listening to reggae. I requested they crank up the volume, which they did until the anesthesiologist insisted they turn it down so he could listen to the rhythm of my heart. My surgeon arrived and it was show time.

I mainlined some narcotics and was out until I woke up six hours later in the recovery room. Except I wasn't in a recovery room, I was in my room. I was expecting to be sharing a room at the Motel 6, but was pleasantly pleased to find myself in a private room at the Plaza.

My attending nurse walked in, introduced herself and printed her name across a dry erase board much as my teachers would do on the first day of school. Like Vanna White, she pointed out the many fine features of my electric bed. She demonstrated the remote control for my flat screen TV, injected me with a generous amount of morphine, handed me my call button, turned down the lights and left. I lay back in my comfy bed and drifted happily off to sleep.

I slept until I was awakened by the return of my nurse. She had stopped by to see how I was doing and I was delighted to discover she was delivering more morphine.

We were engaged in pleasant conversation when, without warning, I erupted like Mount St. Helens and began blowing chunks all over the place. It was as if my mouth had become a fire hose spewing a constant stream of chunky chocolate milk across the length of my bed.

I could not believe the sheer volume and velocity of the liquid I was spewing. I fully expected my head to start spinning around like Linda Blair's in "The Exorcist." I didn't stop puking, hurling, and heaving until I had regurgitated at least a full five percent of my total body weight.

When my performance of peristaltic pyrotechnics concluded my nurse proceeded to clean me up. I was so embarrassed. I immediately began apologizing for my humiliating behavior, but the nurse would have none of it. "No problem," she said, as she continued to clean me up and calm me down. She radioed for assistance and, in short order, my room and I were unsoiled and spotless. I was soon sedated and sleeping.

The following morning, I was greeted by a chipper young man. I immediately became suspicious of his intentions and with good reason. He was my physical therapist and he wanted me to get out of bed and go for a walk with him.

I explained how I had recently had extensive back surgery and suggested perhaps he come back tomorrow. But he chuckled and said, "That was yesterday. It's time for you to get up and start moving."

Next thing I know I'm hobbling in the hallway. We walked down the hall and made a right, and walked down the hall and made a right, and walked down the hall and made a right, another right and we were back where we started. Motherfucker! This was just like gym class!

I would've been pissed except for the sudden realization I'd walked around the entire wing of the hospital without ever stopping to stretch my calves. I had walked around the entire wing of the hospital without suffering any type of pain whatsoever. OMG! I could walk again!

I became extremely emotional and was returned to my bed where I received more morphine, was sedated and slept.

As soon as I awoke I was out the door and cruising the corridors. I had my earbuds in my ears and Snoop Dog blasting on my iPhone. Walking in my hospital gown, I was rocking out with my ass hanging out. I was movin-n-groovin to the rhythm of my pain-free life.

Daytime or nighttime, it didn't matter, if I was awake, I was walking. Around and around I would go, until the hospital staff started looking as familiar to me as I was to them. The nurses would glance up from their computer screens and smile as I strolled by. Sometimes they would wave to me, give me the "thumbs up" or glance at each other as if to say, "Look, it's the old white guy again."

Yes, the hospital was becoming aware of me and I was becoming aware of the hospital. I was becoming aware of the countless ways in which my fellow patients were suffering. I was becoming aware of the sights, sounds, and smells of sadness, desperation and death. And I was becoming acutely aware of how blessed I was to be alive, healthy, and happy.

I was also becoming aware of the way in which the patients treated the hospital staff. I knew they were sick, and I was sure many of them were scared, but some patients treated the nurses like shit. I found their behavior to be most disturbing.

Therefore, whenever anyone entered my room, or I passed them in the hallway, I made sure they understood how grateful I was for everything they were doing for me. I made it my business to thank each and every hospital employee I encountered for the wonderful care I was receiving. I made sure they understood I was aware and appreciative of their efforts.

They say, "What goes around comes around," and things were coming around to me. Everybody working on the floor treated me like a king.

After making its rounds, the meal delivery cart would stop by and provide me with a veritable smorgasbord of fine foods. The kitchen staff stocked my room with a wide variety of fresh fruits, vegetables, dips, drinks, and desserts. Housekeeping brought me extra "everything" and removed the unnecessary furniture from my room so it would be more spacious. The orderlies brought me bouquets of flowers left behind by patients who had checked out.

I was only allowed to receive morphine every four hours and I never had to wait. A few minutes before the four-hour mark arrived, a nurse would magically appear. We would chat as we watched the clock tick down. She would give me my shot and my pill.

I didn't know what the pill was for and I didn't give a shit. Turns out, the pill was a "stool softener" to help me shit.

You see, not only can morphine turn pain into pleasure, but it can also turn your crap into concrete. And after two days in the hospital my bowels were locked up tighter than OJ Simpson. I had to go, but my ass said, "No."

The nurses loaded me up with laxatives hoping to unclog a log. I sat down on the toilet and prayed, but nothing happened. Again, I tell you, it is easier for a camel to pass through the eye of a needle than for a turd to pass through my sphincter.

I pushed and strained and squeezed as hard as I could, trying to blast a colon cannonball out of my bunghole, but couldn't do it. The pain of the strain was becoming too much for me and I began begging for a turd to burst out of my belly like the monster did in "Alien."

Exhausted and soaked in sweat, I was ready to give up when the turtle peaked. A little marble dropped and upon hearing the splash of the pea-sized pellet a smile crossed my lips and hope filled my heart. Another marble dropped, and another, and another, and another until I started shitting gravel. I was doing the teeny tiny turd tango with the toilet and I was so relieved.

I was relieved as well as released. Reluctantly, I was released from the hospital and would now have to go home. I had stayed for four days and although we all knew this day was coming, the realization of its arrival was still difficult for some to take. Rumors of my impending departure spread throughout the floor and my room was soon filled with old friends, well-wishers, and tear-filled eyes.

After putting on my clothes and packing my toothbrush in a pocket, I paused for a moment to take one final look around the room. Many memories returned of days filled with friendship, food, and feces.

How could I forget the first night I puked? Or the morning they removed my catheter? Watching NASCAR with the security guards? Ordering collard greens from "Roscoe's Chicken and Waffles?" The tits on the towel girl, or trading cold cheese sandwiches for green Jell-O? Surely, I'd miss it all. Memories; "like sands through the hourglass, so are the days of our lives."

Looking back on it all I'm filled with a sense of wonder. I wonder where I'd be today if I had not been fortunate enough to have the motorcycle accident. Perhaps I'd be in New Zealand, or perhaps I'd be in a wheelchair. Perhaps I would be an assistant director, or perhaps I would be dead.

I wonder what would've happened if I had not been fortunate enough to lose my job. I wonder what would've happened if we had not elected a Kenya-born, Muslim, Socialist, Mom-jeans wearing, Pussy Dictator to rule over this country?

I wonder what would've happened if a couple in Egypt had not conceived a child who would one day attend Harvard University. What if people in Japan had not created my motorcycle? What if "illegals" had not risked their lives to come and clean my puke off the floor or the turds out of the toilet?

What about the Chinese sweatshop workers who sewed my hospital gown? Or the Africans who mined the minerals which will forever reside inside me? The teachers, brick masons, dockworkers, stockbrokers, cotton pickers, cocksuckers, politicians, prostitutes, priests, bartenders, butchers, bakers and candle stick makers who were all responsible for stabbing me in the back?

What if all the forces of this universe had not conspired to come together so I may experience this life now, in this moment? I wonder.

Although I will always prefer the horizontal over the vertical, thanks to the determination of my Granddaddy Eddins, the knowledge of my loving wife, and the skills of a talented surgeon, I am now able to walk painlessly with poise and grace.

# KEY WEST

After spending five years in college earning a four-year degree in Biology, I ventured down to the Florida Keys with some friends to celebrate graduation and our new-found freedom. After enjoying two wonderful weeks of unfettered drinking, drugs and debauchery, my friends left to go work on their various careers while I remained in Florida to work on my tan.

I soon found myself house sitting a small private island for a man from Michigan. The island was south of Big Pine Key and it had neither electricity nor running water.

His was the only house on the Island and it had been under construction for many, many years. It did not have windows or doors; empty holes in the walls indicated where they would be installed. There wasn't a kitchen or bath so I cooked on a Coleman stove and crapped in the woods. I slept in a sleeping bag on a plywood floor underneath a half-finished roof. I was Robinson Crusoe living on my own island and I loved it.

I had a small boat and motor and before sunset I'd venture out to the coral reef and drop anchor. I'd mix a 5-gallon bucket full of fish heads and guts with sand I'd pilfer from construction sites. Using a large wooden spoon, I'd introduce this mixture into the water. The blood-soaked sand would drift down onto the reef's surface sending the fish into a feeding frenzy.

Using several baited hand lines, I'd pull fish from the ocean all night. I had a thermos full of soup, a thermos full of coffee, a battery-powered radio and the stars above. I was in heaven.

At sunrise, I'd motor over to the wholesale fish warehouse and sell my catch. With my proceeds, I'd purchase the gasoline and bait needed for the following night.

My profits, if there were any, were spent on necessities such as cigarettes, beer, and Cheese Whiz. If necessary, I'd supplement my income by shucking oysters and washing dishes at the Big Pine Inn.

Most of my daytime hours were spent at Bahia Honda State Park. I'd use their facilities to shit, shower and shave. I loved swimming naked in the crystal-clear water and sleeping in the warm, white sand. Quite often there were other naked people frolicking on the beach and we'd spend the day socializing, throwing frisbees and drinking as we baked our bodies in the hot Florida sun.

We would share whatever we had to eat or drink with each other and what we usually had to eat was lobster. Anytime you were hungry, all you had to do was put on your snorkel, swim out a little ways, pick one of the creatures up from the ocean floor, rip its head from its tail, drop the tail in a pot of boiling water and voilà, you've got a meal.

At first, I couldn't believe this. Free lobster! Oh my god, this was fantastic! However, after several months of eating lobster, I discovered it was not so fantastic; it sucked.

We'd prepare lobster stew, lobster and eggs, lobster in Mac N Cheese and lobster with Hamburger Helper. We'd smother it with garlic butter, horseradish, catsup, mustard, Worcestershire sauce and anything else we could find to make it taste like something besides another stinking lobster.

The time I spent living alone on the island was idyllic. It was possibly the most peaceful and carefree time of my life and I shall cherish those days forever. However, I eventually left the little island and moved further south to the big island of Key West. Bright lights! Big City!

Key West is where I began my career in advertising. One day I walked into a local radio station and by using my superior intellect and masterful persuasive skills, I convinced the owner of the station to hire me as a salesman. Looking back on that fateful meeting, I now believe he would've hired basically anyone foolish enough to walk in and ask to be a salesman.

The radio station was called "WKWF" and it sucked ass. It was an automated country and western station. "Automated" means it didn't have actual disk jockeys spinning records at the station. It only had antiquated tape decks playing suck ass Hillbilly music all day long.

WKWF wasn't even an FM station. It was an AM station with a weak signal and in every way imaginable it sucked ass, but I didn't care.

I didn't care, because a few weeks ago I was nothing but a dish-washing, oyster-shucking fisherman. But now I had a business card which said I was an executive. Next thing you know, I'm wearing shoes, a tie, a watch and carrying a briefcase because that's the kind of shit executives do.

Back in those days, Key West was divided into two separate sections. The original section of town was known as "Old Town" and the newer section of town was known as "Sears Town."

Old Town consisted of historical buildings, brick streets, colorful bars and boarded up businesses.

Sears Town consisted of modern motels, car dealerships, chain restaurants and the Sears mall. If there was any money to be made in advertising, it was to be made in Sears Town.

The radio station itself was located on Duvall Street in Old Town. Duvall Street is the main thoroughfare running through the center of Old Town and although it's a mere mile in length, it is known as the "longest street in the world" because it runs from the Atlantic Ocean all the way to the Gulf of Mexico.

Duval Street was home to a few small bars, bodegas and boutiques. There was a Cuban coffee shop, a laundromat and a porn store complete with quarter video booths. The world famous Sloppy Joe's Bar was located on Duvall Street as well as The Monroe Theater, which showed "Deep Throat" and "The Devil and Miss Jones" twice daily for almost a decade. The Miami mafia used the place to launder money.

Duvall was home to hippies, hookers and the homeless. There were crooks and crazies, drunks, druggies and degenerates. These were my people and I instantly felt at home in Old Town.

Old Town was where I wanted to do business, but no one in Old Town wanted to do business with me. No one, and I mean no one, was the least bit interested in buying advertising on an AM country and western radio station. Let me reiterate, WKWF sucked ass.

Day after day, I'd walk up and down Duvall Street going door to door, visiting business after business after business and selling nothing. Week after week I was faced with a demoralizing level of financial failure.

Most men would have given up, thrown in the towel and walked away, but not me. I was not going to quit. No sir, I'd never quit because for me it wasn't a matter of making money, it was more about socializing with the locals and getting laid.

I was having a wonderful time. I knew every business person in Old Town and everybody knew my name. I was a stranger to no one and everyone was my friend. I spent my days drinking beer in the bars, playing backgammon in the bodegas and engaging in a wide variety of luscious and lascivious activities.

I was doing well, but business was bad. I was barely making enough sales to keep from getting fired when things started to change. Rich gay guys from Fire Island were opening businesses and buying homes. A guy called Jimmy Buffett was becoming a star and the radio station began broadcasting "live" for one hour each evening with Frisco Bobby playing jazz.

Soon our little AM station was transmitting live with actual disk jockeys playing a combination of Jimmy Buffet, jazz, reggae and mellow rock. The laid-back rhythm of the island itself merged with this music to create a sound we called "Island Rock." WKWF simply sounded like Key West.

WKWF became the hip station to listen to and Key West became the hip place for the hipsters to vacation. Tourists started flowing into Old Town and money started flowing into my pockets.

Everyone in the business community either knew me or knew of me and I became the go-to-guy for those wanting to buy air time on WKWF.

I would spend my days discussing advertising with clients while lounging poolside at The Pier House. No longer wearing shoes or a tie, I often attended meetings wearing only my Speedo, tanning oil and sunglasses.

My favorite place to talk business was on my sailboat. If I could get a potential client to go out on my boat, they were not coming back to shore until I had a deal.

I spent my nights in the discos dancing till dawn to Donna Summers. I'd sleep during the afternoon and early evening and late at night I'd venture out on my bicycle, moving from party to party and bar to bar throughout the darkness.

Back then the average tourist only visited the island for two days. They'd drive down from Fort Lauderdale or Miami to check out the island and then return the following day. This meant the girls only had one night to party and if they wanted to spend that night with me, I was happy to oblige.

One summer "the girls" became "a girl." I fooled around and fell in love with a beautiful woman who captured my heart. I left Florida to be with her but she left me to be with another.

Eventually, I would return to the island, but things were no longer the same. The AIDS epidemic arrived and some of my friends started to die. One of my closest friends suffered a debilitating stroke; a young girl I often dated took her own life. People I knew in the marijuana importing business were going to jail and I felt the Island was going to hell.

My two-week graduation vacation had lasted for over seven years, but the party was over.

My friends said, "California is the place you ought to be," so I loaded up the truck and I moved to Beverly. Hills that is. Swimming pools, movie stars.

# HUNTING RATS

I have many fond memories of my youth. I believe by growing up in a small town in West Virginia, I was afforded certain opportunities children from the larger metropolitan areas of this country are denied.

I can remember when I was around eleven years old how my Dad and his friends would take me and my friends out to the city dump to shoot rats. These were happy times filled with laughter, camaraderie and the love shared between a father and his son.

This was back before there was anything known as a "landfill." There wasn't an EPA or any rules or regulations for the disposal of garbage. People dumped their garbage into garbage cans, which was dumped into garbage trucks, which delivered the garbage to the garbage dump.

Our city's dump was located on top of a high hill. The garbage trucks would drive to its summit, back up to its edge, open their rear doors and the garbage would cascade down the mountainside.

Sunday was usually the chosen day for our hunt. I'd start the day of death by attending the First United Methodist Church with my family. I sang in the church choir. I didn't enjoy singing in the choir because I can't carry a tune and my voice sounds like shit.

I did, however, enjoy dressing up in the fancy choir robe and standing on stage in front of the congregation, so I'd fake it. I'd pretend to sing by mouthing the words I heard the others singing, while mumbling softly to myself. If I knew the words to the chorus, I'd belt them out as loud as I could. I'd let the words rip and rise up unto the heavens. But any way you look at it, I suck at singing.

After church, my family and I would go to a local restaurant where we would dine and socialize with other "church-going folks." We'd stuff our faces with roast beef, cottage cheese and Jello before returning home and removing our fancy church clothes.

My dad would read the Sunday paper and nap on the living room couch. My sister would read books. My mother would hang up our fancy church clothes, clean and cook. I would do nothing at all.

At six o'clock the family would gather around the kitchen table for Sunday dinner. Sunday dinner usually consisted of fried chicken, mashed potatoes with gravy, corn on the cob, green beans, buttered cornbread, cucumbers, tomatoes, and scallions. We'd drink sweet tea and have chocolate meringue pie for dessert.

After dinner, my dad would nap on the living room couch. My sister would study for school. My mother would clear the dinner table, scrape the dishes, wash the dishes, dry the dishes and clean the kitchen. I would do nothing at all, except sit with my .22 rifle and fantasize about the upcoming hunt.

I owned a 1959 Remington .22 caliber Nylon 66 autoloader. It was a blowback operated, tubular magazine fed semi-automatic rifle which shot the more powerful .22 long rifle bullets. It was loaded through a recess in its plastic stock and the magazine would hold up to fourteen bullets.

The "auto-loading" action meant firing the rifle would open the side chamber and eject the fired cartridge. This action automatically reloaded the gun and it was instantly cocked and ready to be fired again. The four-pound rifle would fire fourteen bullets in rapid succession so it truly was a killing machine.

The time would arrive for the Sunday slaughter and Dad would join Andy and Bill in the cab of Bill's pickup truck and I'd climb into the back with Scooter and Jimbo. Bill would let out the clutch and we'd be on our way to the city dump. Three young boys with smiles on our faces and our Remington autoloaders on our laps.

Arriving at the dump we'd drive around for a few minutes scouting for the perfect place to park. We'd find a large flat area with an unobstructed view of the Killing Fields and the pickup would pull to a stop. We'd climb out of the truck and our dads would explain "The Rules of the Hunt."

We were NEVER to go past "the line of fire." "The line of fire" was an imaginary line drawn between two objects located in front of the truck, such as a discarded stove and an old water heater. We were NEVER to point our guns in any direction other than past "the line of fire." If one of us was out of bullets we were to carefully walk to the front of the truck with our rifle barrel pointed down toward the ground and one of the adults would reload our rifle for us. That was pretty much it. Those were The Rules of the Hunt.

With our rifles fully loaded, Jimbo, Scooter and I would stand side-by-side behind the line of fire. The truck's headlights would be turned off and the six of us would wait silently in the dark. We'd wait, and wait, and wait, listening intently for the sound of rodents moving through the trash. The anticipation would build as the three of us waited patiently for our prey to appear.

You'd hear the faint clink of a can or see some shadowy movements in front of you. One of our fathers would softly whisper "ready" and then yell "NOW!" We'd hit 'em with the truck's high beams and the rats would be momentarily blinded. In that instant, all hell would break loose.

Bam! Bam! Bam! Bam! Bam! Scooter, Jimbo and I would simultaneously open fire, blowing the shit out of anything and everything in front of us. Bam! Bam! Bam! The bullets would fly, the rats would run and we'd have fun. Bam! Bam! Bam! Bam! Bam! We'd shoot forty-two bullets as fast as we could until our rifles were empty and their barrels were warm. Hell yeah! We were shooting varmints!

As our fathers reloaded our rifles, we were allowed to take our flashlights and venture out into the land of discarded crap in search of the dead and wounded. Once our guns had been reloaded the three of us would return to the line of fire, the lights on the truck would go out, and the entire process would begin again.

Our fathers would sit on the hood of the truck unloading a bottle of "Early Times" while the three of us would stand on the firing line unloading our rifles into anything that moved.

Sometimes our dads would take a roll of black electrical tape and tape a flashlight to the barrel of our rifle. The six of us would venture into the rubbish in search of a fat rat or other stuff to shoot. We'd gather up bottles, rotting produce, plastic toys or anything else we could find which would explode into bits when hit with a bullet.

I once spotted a box full of Mason jars high on top of a refrigerator. Standing on my tippy-toes, I could hardly reach it. I tugged on it a little and a nest full of baby rats fell on top of me. I was instantly covered in live rats! I pissed my pants, but no one noticed.

Why our fathers thought it was okay to give three young kids loaded semi-automatic weapons and allow them to wander around in a rat-infested shit-hole full of rusted metal and broken glass I will never understand.

Eventually, we'd run out of ammunition. The hunt would end and we'd reluctantly have to leave this magical place. We'd jump in the truck and race down the mountainside to the Burger Boy Food-a-Rama for shakes, burgers and fries. We'd laugh and make jokes while recounting the evening's adventures and making our plans for the next big hunt.

Hunting rats brought us closer together, until we were no longer fathers and sons; we were six close friends, with an unbreakable bond which lasted until death us do part.

# TENNESSEE WILLIAMS

One night while living in Key West, I received a phone call from a dear friend inviting me to join her for dinner. Her grandparents were hosting a dinner party for playwright and part-time island resident Tennessee Williams. The party was going to be quite the social event and she felt it would be fun if I were to escort her and her girlfriend to the festivities. I accepted her gracious offer.

Mr. Williams was in town for rehearsals of his play, "Will Mr. Merriweather Return from Memphis?" The play was to be presented at the grand opening of the Tennessee Williams Performing Arts Center, located on the campus of Florida Keys Community College. This was a big deal.

Now, ordinarily, I use the actual names of anyone I happen to mention in my stories. However, in this particular case, I shall not. Although one of the two main characters in this story has since passed away, the other still resides on the island and to mention her name could cause her professional problems. This would be a shitty thing for me to do, therefore I shall refer to these two South Florida socialites as "the girls."

My friend suggested the girls pick me up at my home. We could hang out at my place for a little while, thus giving her friend and me a chance to become better acquainted. I thought this to be a splendid idea and began preparing for the upcoming evening's activities.

My roommate paid to have our house cleaned and the grass mowed. I got a haircut, manicure and facial. I purchased a pair of khaki pants and a sport coat and borrowed a tie from my lawyer.

When the ladies arrived, I was taken aback by their magnificent beauty. They were dressed in elegant evening gowns, fashionable shoes and fine jewelry.

Once introductions were completed and pleasantries exchanged, I suggested we retire to the veranda for a cocktail.

As we sat chatting in my newly purchased plastic chairs, I could not take my eyes off my new friend from Miami. I was mesmerized by her aristocratic appearance and air of sophistication. I found her to be fascinating and felt privileged to be in her presence.

Upon finishing our toddies, the three of us climbed into the back of a rented limousine for the short ride to the party. As the car motored along Atlantic Boulevard, I lowered the tinted window and the three of us gazed out upon the moonlit ocean and up into the star-filled sky. We sat in silence, breathing in the fresh salty sea air and enjoying this time of peace and tranquility.

I suggested perhaps we should open the moon-roof so as to better enjoy the view. The girls suggested perhaps we should take a hit of blotter acid so as to better enjoy the party. After a few moments of careful consideration, we decided to do both. The moon-roof slid into its open position as the acid slid beneath our tongues.

I must say I was cutting quite the handsome figure as I walked from the limo sporting a beautiful woman on each arm. We made our grand entrance into the soirée and were soon surrounded by the social elite. Patrons of the arts filled the room, snacking on hors d'oeuvres and sipping champagne.

I was introduced to my host and hostess who in turn introduced me to Tennessee Williams. The grandparents said they were pleased I was able to attend their party. Mr. Williams said nothing at all as he sat slumped over in a chair staring at his shoes.

The girls and I went our separate ways and I began to mingle with the guests. I moved around the room introducing myself and making small talk. I was polite, witty and charming, which is my forte when placed in such a social situation.

It was a lively room filled with the sounds of clinking glasses, camaraderie and good cheer. Everyone was pleased to make my acquaintance and one gentleman even complimented me on my tie.

I flowed along with the other guests as we made our way into the dining room to take our assigned seats at the dinner table. The table itself was magnificent. It was the longest single table I'd ever seen in my life. It was covered with white linens, laid with the finest china, cutlery, and silver candlesticks.

Tennessee Williams, being the guest of honor, took his seat at the head of the table with me seated to his right, although at the absolute opposite end of the table.

Appetizers were served and as I gazed down upon my Duck Pot Au Feu, I realized I had no desire for food. However, my appetite for Tanqueray and tonic was insatiable.

Mr. Williams was now having a wonderful time, filling the room with laughter and clever conversation. I was also having a fine evening, as was everyone seated around the table. This was a joyful celebration of life and I was pleased to be a part of it.

Once the meal was completed, the table was cleared and each guest was presented with coffee and a slice of Key lime pie. Our host rose from his seat and tapped lightly upon his wine glass with a spoon, thus asking for quiet.

As I turned to hear what he had to say, a flock of screeching blue florescent birds came swooping down the table straight at me. They were huge birds with bright blue neon tipped wings and piercing red hot eyes. They were upon me in an instant with their razor-sharp talons fully exposed and ready to rip me to shreds!

I leaped from my seat, screaming the scream of death while beating the beaked bastards off of me with my fist. Diving to the floor, I desperately tried to crawl underneath the table, but it was too late. One of the feathered fuckers landed upon me. Fighting for my life, I ripped a wing from its body, jumped to my feet and stomped its head to bits!

The airborne assholes were fluttering and flapping everywhere and some of the dinner guests were starting to panic. I could see the confusion on their faces and fear in their eyes as I raced past them.

I ran, helter-skelter, around the table, with the big blue beasts squawking, flying and zooming right behind me! I ran out of the room! I ran out of the house! I ran into the street and the birds vanished into the night sky! I looked everywhere, but they were gone.

Collapsing to the curb, I started to cry. I was shaking uncontrollably while holding my head in my hands and trying desperately to catch my breath.

"What the fuck!" "What the fuck!" was all I could say. I kept repeating these words over and over again until I heard a voice respond, "What the fuck?" A second voice chimed in saying, "What the fuck?"

Razing my head from my hands, I looked up to see the girls. They were looking down at me as if to say, "What the fuck?"

The instant our eyes met we started laughing. We laughed and laughed and laughed until the three of us were quite hysterical. Which, as you may know, people under the influence of hallucinogens are quite prone to do.

I refused to go back inside, so the girls brought me a bottle of Kahlúa and a plate of hot wings. I sat quietly on the curb and enjoyed the remainder of the evening.

As the guests were walking out to their cars, I wished them adieu and thanked them all for coming.

# GUTTED

Before my mother died I would make an annual pilgrimage to West Virginia to see her. More often than not I'd visit her at Christmas. Christmas was Mom's favorite time of the year. She loved attending holiday parties with her friends. She loved the Christmas lights, and the Nativity scenes. She loved watching "It's a Wonderful Life" on TV and listening to Bing Crosby singing "White Christmas" on her stereo. Mom loved anything and everything associated with the holiday season, but most of all she loved going to the First United Methodist Church on Christmas Eve. She loved her children and when we were with her it made her Christmas complete.

I enjoyed spending the Christmas holidays at home primarily for the presents, parties and pussy. Between the towns of Bluefield, Princeton and Beckley there are seven bars total. Although the locals would visit their favorite bar in the evening, I'd visit every single speakeasy in every single town every single night.

I'd start my nightly sojourn early in the evening and return to Mom's the next morning. This was my modus operandi. This is what I enjoyed most about Christmas.

Mom always served dinner at five o'clock and it took me about two hours to prepare for the evening's activities. Ordinarily I'd be on the hunt around seven but this particular night I went out early. It must have been early because I found myself all alone in a strip mall bar down on Hamburger Highway before sunset.

I arrived at the establishment wearing a white turtleneck sweater, khaki pants, shined shoes and sporting my trademark tan.

I sat alone in the deserted bar sipping on a margarita and admiring myself in the mirror when the door opened and silhouetted by the sun "She" walked in. She looked stunning and glided effortlessly across the puke-stained carpet as if she were walking down the runway at the Academy Awards.

She sat next to me and introduced herself as Betty Jo or Bobbie Sue or Carol Anne or one of those other two-name names that are popular in that part of the country. I told her my name was Chris. She said she was from Bluefield and I said I was from Beverly Hills. She said she worked at the Celanese plant making cigarette filters and I said I worked in Hollywood making movies. I offered to buy her a drink. I suggested she enjoy a frosty margarita like mine, but she wanted a Stroh's beer. I wanted her, she wanted a can of Stroh's, so I purchased the libation of her choice.

I told her of my worldly travels, show business and how I spent my time with Hollywood stars. It was obvious from my attire and demeanor I was well-educated and had plenty of money. I was witty and charming, but she was not impressed. She was not impressed, that is, until "He" walked in.

He was five-foot two, sporting an orange jumpsuit and a green baseball cap. His hat said, "John Deer" and his teeth said, "I need to see an orthodontist." He sat next to her and introduced himself to us as Joe Bob or Jimmy James or Billy Jack or one of those two-name names that are popular in that part of the country.

Now, I try to be nonjudgmental, but what can I say? This guy looked like shit. He smelled of cigarette smoke, perspiration, and death. He asked the bartender for a "Redeye," which I learned is a combination of beer and tomato juice. As the bartender sat this cold combo concoction in front of him, he quietly mumbled in a slow southern drawl, "Thanks, man. I needed this. I've been gutting deer all day."

The moment those words left his lips, Donna Debbie left me. Her attention was solely upon him.

I tried to continue our conversation, but Bobbie Sue was no longer interested in anything I had to say. She was mesmerized by this man's tales of "Guttin" deer, Bowie knives and bleeding bladders.

"What the fuck?" I thought to myself, "I'm wearing Ralph Lauren and this guy's wearing Bambi's blood."

I watched as they walked arm in arm toward the door. Her tits had been taken away by this man's titillating tales of taxidermy. I sat alone. Dejected, I slowly sipped my Redeye in silence and licked my wounds.

# WHERE ARE YOUR SHOES?

One day I was walking on Rodeo Drive when I was stopped by a heavily armed security guard standing in front of Cartier. "Excuse me sir, but do you know where you are?" he inquired of me. I looked around to reassure myself of my location before answering his question. "I'm in Beverly Hills, California," I answered. "So where are your shoes?" he asked.

"Where are your shoes?" he asked, for the second time as we both glanced down at my bare feet. "Shoes? Why would I be wearing shoes?" I asked him somewhat confused.

"You are walking on Rodeo Drive, sir. This is one of the most exclusive shopping areas in the world and you're not wearing any shoes," he said in a somewhat condescending manner. "I'm not wearing any underwear, so why would I be wearing shoes?" I replied in a somewhat fuck-you manner.

"I'm not shopping on Rodeo Drive. I'm only walking on Rodeo Drive. I'm currently on my way to Beverly Drive

where I shall be shopping at the 76 Gas Station for cigarettes." I said, with an air of worldly sophistication.

"Do you see those shoes?" I inquired as I pointed down
at his highly polished footwear. "My bare feet will be taking
me anywhere I choose to go throughout this fine city today
while those shoes will be spending the entire day standing
in front of this store." "Au revoir," I called out over my shoulder as I waved and sauntered away.

I seldom wear shoes. I have never been fond of wearing
shoes and hopefully I'll never have to wear them on a daily
basis. Men who wear shoes and hats are neither connected
to the earth beneath them nor the heavens above.

Quite frankly, I'm not particularly fond of wearing
clothing of any type. I don't wear clothes when I'm in my
home and I try to wear as little clothing as possible when
I'm out in public. Although I exhibit a sense of style, I care
not for fashion.

Some people believe I go shoeless because I was born
and raised in West Virginia. I find this generalization of
my home state to be extremely offensive. Many people believe all Mountaineers to be shoeless fools. This is not true.
However, in my particular case their assumption is correct.

I'm amazed by the number of people who will stop me
to express concern for my feet. "Aren't you afraid of cutting your feet on something?" they will ask. "Aren't your feet
cold?" "Aren't your feet hot?" "Aren't your feet getting wet?"
"Aren't you smart enough to put some fucking shoes on?"

So, if you'll "bare" with me for a few minutes I'd like
to share some information with you concerning my feet.
Hopefully, this will answer many of the questions you may
have on this subject.

The most frequent question I receive is, "Aren't you afraid of cutting your feet on something?"

No, I'm not afraid of stepping on some object and cutting my feet. I tread lightly when I walk. The bottoms of my feet are extremely sensitive, so the moment they detect any sign of possible pain they recoil immediately. It's truly a knee-jerk reaction.

Because the bottoms of my feet are so soft and supple, any small object I may happen to step upon will produce a momentary indention into the malleable skin. The possible hazard is absorbed into the spongy softness of the foot as my weight is supported by the area surrounding the object, thus preventing it from producing enough upward pressure to puncture my impressible foot.

This is not to say small shards of glass and metal do not get stuck in the bottoms of my feet. However, on the rare occasion when this does occur, they are usually removed by simply wiping the bottom of my foot with my hand.

Although, in all honesty, I must admit I once cut a foot badly enough to require "medical" attention. I was the assistant director on a television show which was filming in a downtown LA alley. As usual, I was barefoot and when I jumped behind a dumpster to take a quick piss, I sliced my foot open on a broken bottle.

Our wardrobe girl cleaned out my wound with some hydrogen-peroxide as our prop master sealed the bleeding gash with Superglue. That was the end of that. My foot was fixed. Superglue: "Bonds skin instantly."

I will now expand upon this subject by answering the question, "Why are the bottoms of your feet so pink and soft?"

Most people assume my peds are covered with thick calluses, but this is not the case. Although there is a layer of slightly thicker skin on the outer ball and heel of my feet, for the most part they remain soft and supple. In fact, the insoles of my feet are as soft as a baby's butt. A very wrinkled sixty-four-year-old baby's butt, but a soft one all the same.

When someone wants to remove a callus from their feet they get out a pumice stone or an emery board and "file" the crusty skin off. Everything I walk upon is scrubbing and scraping calluses away before they even get a chance to form. Not only is the surface of concrete and asphalt keeping my feet soft and smooth, walking on things like rocks and gravel give me a free foot massage. It is the wearing of shoes which causes calluses and corns.

"Aren't your feet hot?" is a question I often receive as I stroll calmly around the swimming pool in 100° heat.

People assume because the asphalt, concrete or pool tiles are blistering hot my feet are roasting. It's true my feet may be warm, but they are certainly not "roasting" or "burning" as I move upon a sizzling surface.

The key to this is to pick up your feet as you walk. The moment you raise a foot in the air it starts to cool. So, raise your feet higher than you normally would when walking on a hot surface. Give your foot time to cool before switching off to the warmer one. Do not frantically dance around as this is counterproductive and makes you look idiotic.

"No shirt, No shoes, No service" is "No problem." I've developed several techniques for avoiding this rule and I'll share the most basic of these with you now.

When entering a restaurant without footwear, I walk into the establishment behind someone or a group of people, thus hiding the fact I have no shoes. I leave the group at an opportune time and hasten to a corner booth or table against a wall where my bare feet will be out of view of my server. Once my meal has been delivered I'm home free. Few, if any, restaurants will ask you to leave once you owe them money.

Shopping while barefoot in such places as Trader Joe's, Ace Hardware or Walmart require a much different technique. Of course, I'd never actually shop at Walmart. I'm only using them here as an example.

When stopped by an employee of such an establishment and informed they do not allow shoeless shit heads to shop there, I listen intently while nodding my head in agreement. With a large smile upon my face, I start talking to them in a foreign language. I pretend not to understand what they're talking about, but I'm a nice guy and in total agreement with whatever they may be saying. I make hand and facial gestures showing my appreciation for their help, thank them in my nonexistent language and simply walk away. Few minimum-wage workers will make the effort to fuck with such a friendly foreigner.

Another technique I find to be of use is one I refer to as, "The cut and run." When approached by a security guard or employee, I make it quite apparent I'd love to stop and chat with them, but I don't have the time. I convey to them, "Yes, I'm aware I'm not wearing any shoes but I'm in an extreme hurry and I'll only be in your establishment for a few moments." "I'm just going to quickly grab some beer and then I'll be leaving immediately and forever." I'm just grabbing some eggs! I'm just grabbing a screwdriver! I'm just grabbing my balls! Whatever, the key to this technique is to keep moving and not allow them to pin you down.

The biggest advantage I have when moving around shoeless in public places is the fact that I'm old and white. Once I reached a certain age, I became virtually invisible. This is a fact and I take full advantage of it.

Most people are not only unaware I'm not wearing shoes, they're unaware I even exist. I could probably walk barefoot through our local mall with a head full of acid and a gun in the pocket of my bathrobe and no one would pay any attention to me. I'm just another old white guy.

I've also reached an age where those who do acknowledge my existence don't want to have to deal with my presence. This is a fact and I take full advantage of it.

I can't tell you the number of times I've been pulled over by the police on my motorcycle for excessive speed or reckless riding. They're upon me with their sirens blaring and lights flashing, ready to haul me off to the hoosegow. However, the moment I remove my full-face helmet I can see the disappointment in their eyes. They thought they'd nabbed a young kid, or better yet some minority, but I'm just another old white guy.

Many times, they don't even bother asking for my driver's license and proof of insurance. They'll tell me to slow down before someone gets hurt and they'll leave.

If you like, I'd be happy to pontificate upon my disdain for underwear and hats in the future.

# THE HARD HIT

On Sunday mornings, my wife will usually go to a Yoga class and I'll go on a motorcycle ride. Both of these are forms of relaxation, they quiet the mind and renew the soul.

For me, riding my motorcycle is much like those dreams you have where you're flying. The ones in which you are weightless and soaring effortlessly through the sky. You'll gently lean to your left and start gliding left and you'll lean a little to your right and glide over to your right. You are no longer bound to this earth and you're free.

When riding my motorcycle there's approximately a two-inch patch of rubber keeping me connected to this earth. My hands and butt cheeks are the only things keeping me connected to the machine. If I lean to my left, I go left. If I lean to my right, I go right. With my head enclosed within my full-face helmet I'm alone and flying close to the ground. I am free.

One sunny Sunday I filled my bike full of gas and myself full of coffee and headed out Mulholland Highway towards "County Line." County Line is the place where Los Angeles County and Ventura County meet, thus the name, "County Line." Pretty clever, huh?

Riding the two-lane Mulholland Highway through the twist and turns, hills and valleys of the Santa Monica Mountains is beyond belief. It's as if Walt Disney and God got stoned one day and built a playground for bikers.

Cruising along the mountain's ridge line the sky was clear and crystal blue. Looking to my left I could see sweeping vistas of the California coast and on my right, were panoramic views of the beautiful San Fernando Valley. After an hour's ride, I was able to look down the mountainside and see County Line Beach.

Across the highway from the beach there's a restaurant called "Neptune's Net." It's a famous biker hang out and on Sundays it's packed with the most eclectic group of people you will find anywhere. It's a place where people of all different nationalities, ages, social standings, backgrounds and beliefs come together to share a common bond: "the motorcycle."

On Sundays, everyone from Hollywood celebrities to Hell's Angels will stop by to say, "HI." When I arrived, the place was a rockin & a rollin with around one hundred happy bikers clogging up their arteries and assassinating their livers.

I walked up to the "To Go" window and ordered what I always order, a pulled pork sandwich with fries and a frosty cold 25oz. can of Bud Light. Some people give me a hard time for drinking "Bud Light," but when it comes to beer,

I'm into quantity not quality. I grabbed my tasty-licious lunch and walked over to the beach.

County Line Beach is a wonderful white sandy beach full of suave surfers and nearly naked nubile nymphs, but a quarter mile farther up the coast is a crappy rock-covered beach full of no one. I chose the crappy beach because there was a better chance of being alone and a lesser chance of being incarcerated for consuming an alcoholic beverage in public.

I found a comfortable rock close to the cliff side and lay my banquet out on the boulder before me. Ah, the sun, the surf, the sweet ocean breeze; the serenity and solitude I was seeking. It was perfect, but paradise was lost when I detected some movement on the beach.

"Oh crap, he saw me!" I said to myself. "Now the bastard's coming over here and I'm going to have to put up with his shit." Man, this was a downer. I'm as happy to see a seagull appear on the beach as I'd be to see a herpes sore appear on my lip.

Seagulls, what can I say? Perhaps these birds are best described by the words written in the classic American novel "Jonathan Livingston Seagull," which says, "Most gulls don't bother to learn more than the simplest facts of flight; how to get from shore to food and back again. For most gulls, it is not flying that matters, but eating." Or, perhaps these birds are best described by the words I'm writing now: "They're just flying rats that don't give a shit about anything except for eating shit!"

So, this scavenger flies up the beach and lands a few feet away from me. He stands there giving me that evil sideways glance with his beady little black eye. I was going to give him a french fry if he'd keep quiet, but the stool pigeon ratted me out. He caw-caw-caw-cawed his friends! The blab-blab-blab-blab-blab-blabbermouth cawed everyone!

Soon the sky was full of the beaked bastards, like those flying monkeys in the Wizard of Oz. They had spotted my food and this put me in a fowl mood. They began circling around me in the sky. Squeaking and squawking and diving and swooping; they came at me to see how I'd react, test my boundaries and see how close they could get to my food.

One of them jetted over and fired a turd torpedo at me and his black-and-white snotty poop splashed across my sandwich. Motherfucker! That's it! This shit just got real! They'd crossed a line in the sand and this meant war!

I threw my shit-stained sandwich a few feet in front of me and began collecting a shitload of golf ball sized rocks. The gulls landed a safe distance away and took up their battle positions on top of the larger boulders covering the shore. There was silence as they stood waiting to attack and I sat motionless with a round rock at the ready. Time was on their side but I had an unlimited supply of ammunition.

It was a tense shituation. It was a Mexican standoff. It was just a matter of who would blink first. And of course, the birds did because they blink all the time.

Slowly they began to move toward me and tighten their formation. I tossed them a french fry, giving them false hope and luring them into rock range. Closer and closer they crept. Inch by inch. Step by step. I fired!

My rock rocket ricocheted violently from boulder to boulder, shooting among them and scattering them high into the sky. They flew away squawking in fear and confusion but soon returned and another battle line was formed.

Although I have great distain for these asshats, I must give them credit for their sticktoitiveness. I commend them for their dogged determination. They're persistent little peckers who never give up and I respect them for their tenacity.

One fearless feathered fucker flew in to grab my sandwich and BAM! I nailed the barnstorming bastard in the head and blasted him clean out of the sky! I mean, BAM! I bashed him right upside the head and the sucker went down faster than a priest on a choirboy!

WOW! I leapt to my feet! I couldn't believe it! I mean, what are the odds of hitting a flying bird in the head with a two-inch stone? I didn't kill it; I wasn't trying to. But, I did blow its ass out of the air. This was awesome!

I got so excited I started screaming "Hey, Jonathan Livingston! Come back here and suck my cock you chicken!" as the winged warrior recovered and flew away. "Come back here you turkey!" I shouted while shooting him "the bird."

I marched triumphantly back to the restaurant and shared the story of my grand slam victory with my friends. Yes, this was another feather in my cap and I proudly basked in the glory of my superiority.

Word quickly spread of my aviarian adventure and I was congratulated by many manly men; however, I started to pick up some negative vibes from a couple of the ladies and decided perhaps it was time for me to leave. I said my goodbyes, got on my bike, and headed for home.

I wasn't in much of a hurry, but I'd made a commitment to myself to spend some time working on my tan. Although my battle with the birds had delayed me a bit, if I got home soon there would still be enough quality sun left to fulfill my commitment.

I was now less than five miles from home and I'd ridden this section of Mulholland many times. I'm familiar with every single twist and turn in the road so I cranked on the throttle a little and let-it-roll.

Soon I was motoring along at an enjoyable clip. It was not too fast and not too slow. Like Goldilocks said, "Ahhh, this porridge is just right," and she ate it all up. Well, my speed was just right and I was chewing up some serious concrete at a pretty good pace.

I was cruising along and singing "Born to be Wild" in my head when something horrible happened. I started to sing "It's a Small World." Seriously, I was singing, "It's a world of laughter, a world of tears. It's a world of hopes and . . ." what the hell? The song was stuck in my head and I couldn't stop singing it! "It's a small world after all, it's a small world after all, it's a small . . . ." AAHHHH!!!

I was zooming around a long sweeping right hand turn singing, "It's a Small World" when BAM! There was a huge explosion in front of me and shrapnel was flying everywhere. I slammed on my brakes and slid to a stop.

I didn't see what had happened but there was a smoldering car in the road and a Toyota 4 x 4 lying upside down in a nearby ditch. The car was a Dodge Viper convertible and it had simply disintegrated.

I started running and when I got to the driver's side door I saw a large man who was pinned behind the steering wheel. He was bleeding and screaming and thrashing around.

When I got to the passenger side door, there was no door and I saw a teenage girl who was missing her right arm. She was bleeding profusely and one of her feet was lying in her lap. She was neither screaming nor thrashing around. I was looking down at her and she was looking up at me. It was surreal. I was frozen. I was staring at her and she was staring at me. Sometimes she'd glance around, but she was very aware I was there.

Suddenly a man shoved me out of the way, pulled the baseball cap off her head and began looking at her while holding her eyes open with his fingers. I picked up the hat and moved a few feet away.

People were running everywhere yelling into their cell phones and at each other. The man who pushed me aside was now attending to the man behind the steering wheel. The girl was dead and someone covered her up with a SpongeBob beach towel.

As I type this I'm wearing a blue Nike baseball cap. I'm wearing her hat. I've been wearing the hat for years now. I used to say I was wearing it for her, but I actually wear it for me.

I wear it to remind myself of how blessed I am to be alive. I wear it to remind myself of how fragile life is and to not take it for granted. I wear it to remind myself that in a nanosecond I could be looking up at a stranger who is watching me die.

# WINNERS DON'T QUIT

I started smoking cigarettes when I was sixteen years old. I started smoking because I thought it made me look cool. Of course, my image was everything to me at that age because I had no idea who I was.

The first time I smoked a cigarette it made me sick. It made me nauseous, dizzy and gave me a headache. Everyone feels sick the first time they smoke a cigarette because it's your body's way of saying, "Hey moron, this shit is poison!" But I didn't listen, I just kept puffing away until one day I was able to squelch my body's cries for self-survival.

It's like the first time I drank alcohol it made me sick. It may have been "Everclear" when it went down, but it was every color when it came back up!

It's like the first time I smoked marijuana it made me sick. No, actually it didn't make me sick. It made me cough a couple of times, but other than that, the first time I smoked marijuana was awesome!

Remember the first time you smoked pot? Yeah, I don't either. But I'm sure it was "awesome" because it's always awesome. However, I can't remember the first time I smoked it. Hell, I can't even remember last Wednesday, but luckily, I don't have to. I have an iPhone which remembers everything I need to know and my wife does all my thinking for me. Perfect!

Of course, I don't smoke marijuana anymore. Knowing what I know now, I'd be a fool to still be smoking pot. Why would I smoke that nasty ass stuff when I can eat yummy cannabis cakes, cookies, brownies, lollipops and juju thingies?

These kids today have it made. Why, back when I was growing up we didn't have marijuana stores on every corner. No sir, we had to walk miles to some dangerous dorm room or out of a bar and into the parking lot to get our marijuana!

You couldn't even buy pre-rolled joints back when I was young! We had to roll our own! I'm not kidding, there was no one to do the work for us, we had to roll up our sleeves, get our hands dirty and roll our own. Why, I can remember when I'd roll joints until my fingers were rubbed raw and my tongue would be covered in bloody paper cuts from licking the glue on the rolling papers!

Things sure have changed. Back in the day, I'd get stoned, get the munchies and eat tasty things. Now, I just eat tasty things and get stoned. I no longer have to spend all that time smoking pot to get the munchies; I go straight to the munchies.

I love the new edibles but there's a big difference between eating marijuana and smoking it. When you smoke it you can generally get your act together momentarily if you have too. You know, like if the cops are knocking on the door or the baby falls off the bed or something like that. But when you're stoned on edibles there's no coming back. When you eat the right amount it's wonderful but when you eat too much you're fucked. When you cross that line there's no coming back. Proceed with caution.

Writing about herbal refreshments has made me so hungry I want to grab a brownie from the refrigerator. It's so tempting, but if I eat it I may not be able to write, right? I'm in a culinary quandary. It's a Catch-22 or one of those enigma thingies.

I must press on. Back to writing about cigarettes.

Like I said, I started smoking cigarettes when I was sixteen. I started smoking because it was a rite of passage toward adulthood. Smoking, alcohol, drugs, and sexual intercourse were all perceived as rites of passage, and fortunately for me, I was able to reach full adulthood by spending only one weekend in Myrtle Beach, South Carolina.

You need to understand this was way, way back in 1968 and back then everybody smoked.

"More doctors smoke Camels than any other cigarette" was a popular advertising campaign at the time and my doctor smoked! My dentist smoked. My grandfather, my grandmother, my pastor, my teachers, my parents' friends and my parents' friends' friends all smoked cigarettes.

There was hardly a home in West Virginia which didn't have a coffee table with a great big fancy ashtray sitting on top of it. These things were status symbols. Sometimes people would have an ashtray on every flat surface in every room of their house.

Why, even cars had ashtrays in them. Seriously, automobile manufacturers built cars with ashtrays in the dash and the doors. And not only did the cars come with multiple ashtrays, but the ashtrays came with little electric cigarette lighters in them.

My mother drove a Lincoln Continental Town Car which had four ashtrays in it. It was a luxury automobile so everybody had their own personal ashtray and each ashtray came equipped with an electric cigarette lighter. This was necessary because the car's interior was so large that if it had come with only one ashtray a person's arm may not have been long enough to reach it.

Back in those days people used to read newspapers and those things were chock full of cigarette ads. In fact, cigarette ads were everywhere. There were cigarette ads in schools, restaurants, and movie theaters. Hell, not only were people allowed to smoke in the lobby of movie theaters, the people in the movie itself were smoking cigarettes.

There were even cigarette ads on TV! Television commercials where doctors and celebrities would encourage people to start smoking, particularly children and teens. The commercials would tell people they could be as happy, attractive and "cool" as the people in the commercials if they smoked a particular brand of cigarettes. And these ads worked because around forty-five percent of all Americans smoked cigarettes in the Sixties.

Back when I was a young child my favorite TV show was a cartoon called "The Flintstones." It was a show about comical cavemen, women and talking dinosaurs and all of the cartoon characters in the show smoked "Winstone" cigarettes.

When I a youngster, I would sit on my granddaddy's lap and we'd watch a show called "Gunsmoke." The show was sponsored by Marlboro cigarettes and I wanted to be the "The Marlboro Man" when I grew up. The Marlboro Man was this cowboy who rode around on a huge stud horse. He always had a cigarette hanging out of his mouth and a long, stiff saddle horn sticking out of his crotch. He even had his own country, "Marlboro Country," and I knew he was screwing every girl living there.

When I was a freshman in college, a pack of cigarettes only cost twenty-six cents. I know you may find this hard to believe, but it's true. I went to college. Not only did I go to college, but I attended college in Burlington, North Carolina. I'm sure all of you know Burlington is "The Sock Capital of the World," but did you also know it's located in the heart of tobacco country? Well, it is, and as part of my freshman orientation, I could get cartons of cigarettes for free. That's right, free cigarettes! They'd give the freshmen students lots of free cigarettes and all the students had to do was to give the tobacco companies money for the rest of their shortened lives.

I became addicted to masturbation immediately and it didn't take me much longer than that to become hooked on cigarettes. And when I say I was "hooked" on cigarettes I mean I was HOOKED! For over thirty-five years I smoked at least a pack or two every day. So, let's see now, how many would that be? 20 x 365 x 35 = a shit load of cigarettes.

The first thing I did when I woke up in the morning was to lie in bed and smoke a couple of butts. I'd smoke one in the shower and another one while brushing my teeth. For the rest of the day, whatever I was doing, I'd smoke while doing it until I could take a break from doing it and go have a smoke.

I couldn't drink a cup of coffee, make a phone call, start my car, or make a decision without first having a cigarette. I was an addict and tobacco was my drug of abuse. I mean, it's quite common for a man to smoke after sex, but I smoked during sex. I kid you not, I'd stop getting ass to get a butt!

When I was an assistant director on the Power Rangers I'd leave for location around five in the morning. I'd stop at 7-Eleven and buy two packs of cigarettes and 53oz. Big Gulp filled with ice coffee. I'd suck coffee through a straw and chain-smoke cigarettes while racing to the film set. As soon as I'd arrive, my assistant would bring me the script we were shooting, a pack of cigarettes, and a Redbull.

I've never had much of an interest in food and only ate it as a way to stay alive. Usually I didn't want to stop whatever it was I was doing long enough to eat. I'd constantly skip meals and rely on cigarettes to suppress my appetite and caffeine to keep me going. I lived on cigarettes and Coca-Colas. Many people are unaware the human body can subsist solely on cigarettes if you supplement them with caffeine.

I was killing myself slowly, but a day came when smoking nearly killed me.

On September 3, 2001, a friend of mine died in a car accident. Her name was Thuy Trang and she was the actress who played the part of the Yellow Ranger on the original Power Rangers TV show. She was young, talented and a beautiful person in every sense of the word. Thuy was also a Buddhist. She was cremated on September 10, 2001, and two of my friends and I attended her service.

Of course, I'd been to funerals before, but they were for Baptists, not Buddhists. Baptist funerals are simple. You go to the church, you sing a few songs, the preacher preaches, you drop the casket in a hole and go eat fried chicken and potato salad. Simple.

Thuy's service was not simple. There were lots of Buddhist monks involved and they burned incense, rang bells and banged gongs. They'd chant, sing and pray and Thuy's family, friends, and fellow thespians would stand before her altar and speak.

Each testimonial was followed by more bell ringing, gong banging, chanting, singing, and praying. This kept going on and on and on forever and some people desperately wanted to go outside and have a cigarette, but not me. I was wearing a nicotine patch. In fact, I was wearing two nicotine patches because that's how I roll.

At the time, I was wearing nicotine patches in an attempt to get off cigarettes and I hadn't smoked one in months. The patch was designed to release nicotine into my system through my skin, thus suppressing my need to smoke. I can't remember how long one was supposed to last, but I slapped a second one on to make sure I was covered for the entire service. I'm sure glad I did because the thing was lasting longer than the Super Bowl. Including the pre- and post-game shows.

At long last the time arrived for everyone to form a procession and carry Thuy's casket to the crematorium. My friends and I decided this was a good time for us to form a procession and carry our tired asses home.

While riding back to Los Angeles the three of us shared stories of working with Thuy and although we did laugh a little, for me it was a sad affair. Eventually our conversations ended and we sat in silence as we motored along the freeway.

I was in the backseat watching my friends smoking in the front when I started thinking how nice it would be to have a cigarette. Perhaps I should have one to help me unwind after the long, emotional day I'd had. The words "Can I bum a smoke?" escaped my lips and a pack landed in the back. I picked it up, lit one up and that was that. I smoked over half the pack before they dropped me off at my place.

The moment I walked through the front door I hit the floor. I had a seizure. I was having violent muscle spasms and couldn't stop banging the back of my head over and over again against the hard, wooden floor. I was sweating profusely, vomiting and shaking uncontrollably. I began slipping in and out of consciousness and died.

No, I didn't die. I'm only kidding, but I did come damn close! I was in the final stages of nicotine poisoning and could've suffered respiratory failure and gone into a coma.

The warning label says, "(NEVER ever use nicotine patches other than as directed and DO NOT combine smoking when using them!)" I wasn't smoking while wearing a nicotine patch, I was chain-smoking while wearing two of them! Sometimes I'm amazed by the sheer depth of my limitless stupidity.

Most lethal doses of nicotine will kill you within the first hour of poisoning, but like I said earlier, "I didn't die." Maybe I didn't die, but oh my god it would've been merciful. I couldn't control my body temperature and would shiver and shake as if I were freezing. I'd clench my jaw and grind my teeth and my muscles would lock up to the point where I became rigid and unable to move. My vision was blurry, I had difficulty breathing and my speech was slurred. I was seriously fucked up.

I awoke to find my wife shaking me and saying some people were flying planes into buildings or some shit like that. I told her, "I don't care what they're doing! Go away! Leave me alone!" It was 9/11/2001 and I slept through it all.

Once again, my body was saying, "Hey moron, this shit is poison!" And, hello! This time I listened. This time I got the message loud and clear. This was it! I was absolutely done with cigarettes!

I was done, except for the fact I couldn't stop smoking them. I'd tried so many times and so many ways to quit, but I'd always fail. I have an endless list of things at which I have failed in my life, and quitting smoking is near the top of the list. Failure is my forte.

I once joined a stop smoking program similar to Alcoholics Anonymous. The meetings were much like AA meetings except when we'd take a break we wouldn't go outside to smoke, we'd go outside and drink.

I'd stand before a room full of wheezing, coughing, blue-lipped smokers and tell them how cigarettes were destroying my life. Everybody liked my stories the best because I'd just make shit up so the meetings wouldn't be so boring.

This was one of those twelve-step programs where you have a sponsor who's an ex-smoker to help you overcome your addiction. So, whenever I was suffering from nicotine withdrawal or wanted to smoke, I'd call my sponsor for moral support. She did her absolute best to help me, but soon we were having sex and she started smoking again.

I went to a hypnotist who had an office filled with all kinds of spiritual artifacts, multi-colored crystals, pyramids and paintings. I settled back onto a comfy chaise lounge next to a bubbling waterfall and listened to tranquil music as wind chimes blew softly outside the window.

The hypnotist spoke to me in gentle, soothing tones. He told me to close my eyes, relax and release any tension I was holding in my body. To clear my mind of any thoughts and listen only to the sound of his voice. But, I couldn't concentrate on the sound of his voice because all I could hear was the bubbling waterfall and I desperately needed to take a piss.

I tried an acupuncturist. He stuck needles into my ears and it worked. I immediately stopped smoking! However, I required acupuncture every week and it was costing me a fortune. When he stopped shoving needles into my ears, I started shoving cigarettes into my mouth.

I also tried "Nicorette." Nicorette was the first nicotine replacement product on the market. It was a gum which contained nicotine. I'd chew it to decrease the withdrawal symptoms I'd experience when I would stop smoking. I chewed a lot of Nicorette and when I couldn't get the gum, I'd smoke cigarettes to decrease the withdrawal symptoms I experienced when I'd stop chewing.

People who have never smoked have no idea how addicting cigarettes are. An addiction is an addiction and getting off heroin is easier than getting off cigarettes. People will say, "Oh, he needs help, he's a heroin addict." Well, fuck him! Heroin is nothing compared to cigarettes!

Cigarette smokers are not only addicted to the nicotine, but they're also fighting the even stronger addiction to refined sucrose! Cigarettes are packed full of sugar. You light up a cigarette and you're smoking a candy bar. Smoke sugar all day long for years and see how easy it is to stop that shit! Seriously!

Cigarettes suck, and I was destined to suck cigarettes until the day I died. When, through the grace of God, I happened to meet a little old lady who told me, "Quitting's easy. Get me a piece of paper and a pencil and I'll teach you how."

She said, "This takes four weeks so you're going to quit on March fifth." She told me to write this down: "March fifth, two thousand and two, I will stop smoking forever." She told me to say these <u>exact</u> words three times as soon as I awoke in the morning and to say them three times at night right before going to sleep. I was also told to say them three times anytime I became aware I was saying them to myself.

She said, "On March fifth, two thousand and two, don't smoke." She said whenever I wanted a cigarette to say, "March fifth, two thousand and two, I *stopped* smoking forever." She said to say these exact words to myself three times and by the time I said this to myself the urge to smoke will have passed and I'd have reinforced in my mind the fact that I no longer smoked.

The little old lady said, "That's it. That's how you quit." And I said, "That's it? That's how you quit? Are you kidding me? I'm going to click my heels together three times and say, 'there's no place like home,' and stop smoking? Are you fucking kidding me? Shut the fuck up lady! Shut the fuck up!"

Okay, so I didn't actually say that to her. But you can bet your ass that's what I was thinking! What I really said was, "Well, thank you ma'am. I appreciate your help."

She told me it had worked for her and she "likes helping other people to quit." She said she read about it in "The Readers Digest." And I said, "The Readers Digest! Are you fucking kidding me? The fucking Readers Digest! Shut the fuck up, lady! Shut the fuck up!" Okay, so I didn't actually say that to the little old lady. I didn't say anything at all, I only smiled.

Before going to sleep that night, I said, "March fifth, two thousand and two, I will stop smoking forever." I said it three times and I said it again as soon as I awoke.

One day I became aware of saying it to myself while I was waiting at a traffic light so I said it three times. I said it while I was standing at a urinal. While I was riding in an elevator. When I was washing dishes, tying my shoes, taking out the trash, waiting in the checkout line. When I was sitting, standing, lying down and walking around. Anytime my mind would take a mental break these words would pop into my head and I'd have to say them three times. It was like one of those songs you get stuck in your head and you can't stop singing it over and over again to yourself.

By the end of the third week I was like, "Let's get this shit over with already!" I wanted it to stop but I couldn't stop! I wouldn't stop! There was no way in hell I was going to stop saying it until March fifth, two thousand and two, and when I did stop saying it, I was going to stop smoking forever!

I didn't cut back on the number of cigarettes I smoked. I didn't change any of my smoking habits. March fourth, I smoked just like I'd always smoked. I didn't chew the gum or use the patch or stick needles in my ears or anything! I did everything exactly like I'd always done except on March fifth, two thousand and two, I didn't smoke.

BUT OH MY GOD I WANTED TO SMOKE! I've never wanted anything so much in my life! I needed a cigarette! I was freaking the fuck out and climbing the walls! I wanted a cigarette and I wanted it now! I wanted one to the very core of my being, but I'd come this far and every time I wanted to smoke I'd tell myself, "March fifth, two thousand and two, I *stopped* smoking forever." I said it one time. I said it two times. I said it three times. I said it three times, every time I wanted a cigarette and I said it over and over and over again for the whole damn day! And I didn't smoke.

March fifth, two thousand and two, I stopped smoking forever. I haven't had one cigarette since. I'm only telling you this because I like helping other people to quit.

# GOING HOME

When I die, there will be flames and twisted metal. Crowds will gather, drawn to the site of my demise by the smoldering embers, emergency vehicles, and flashing lights.

Women will cry and cover children's eyes. Men will talk among themselves saying such things as, "What the hell was he thinking?" and "Another couple of inches and he probably could've made it." My life will have ended and my long journey home will have begun.

My charred remains will be scraped up, collected and placed into an ambulance for the slow ride to the morgue. There'll be no need for screaming sirens as I will have already reached my destination. There'll be no service, no flowers, no friends.

I will be cremated with my two most valued possessions. A little stuffed dog I received when I was four years old and which has remained faithfully by my side for all these many years. My wedding ring, the gold band which represents the limitless love I have been so blessed to receive.

To know at one point in your life, if only for one brief moment in your life, that you were not alone in this life, to me that makes life worth living.

My adoring wife will transport the cardboard box containing the plastic bag with my final remains to the Florida Keys. There I will be placed into a short, thick section of steel pipe which will be unceremoniously welded shut.

My wife and two trusted friends will sail across the warm, crystal clear waters of the Florida Keys to the old abandoned light house off the Key West shore.

Here, I shall be secured as high as possible onto this amazing steel structure. Here, I shall remain basking in the sun which warmed me in my youth. Here, I shall remain elevated above the ocean I love. Here I shall endure the hurricane's wind, thunder, lightning and rain.

Here, I shall rest for a long, long time. However, rust never sleeps and eventually holes will appear in my home above the sea. Ever so slowly I will be released unto the wind and water. I will be carried far and wide to places unknown. What a glorious trip it shall be.

## THE END

# INTRODUCTION TO
# MY NEXT BOOK

# COMING ATTRACTIONS

*"Freedom is just another word for nothing
left to lose"*

*— Janis Joplin*

It was Christmas Eve and I'd just shit my pants. I was curled up in a fetal position, sobbing uncontrollably and utterly alone in this life. I was physically, mentally and emotionally exhausted. I was shattered. I was lost.

I'd lost my wife. I'd lost my home, my job, my money and my mind. If it weren't for the 250 mg of Lamotrigine I take every morning I probably would have lost my life. I wasn't having a very good day.

Christmas sucked! It sucked because it reminded me of all the wonderful times I'd had as a child. It took me back to those magical days of innocence and wonder.

As a child, I couldn't wait for Christmas Day to arrive, and now I couldn't wait for it to be over. Christmas reminded me of all the bad decisions I'd made in my life. All the wonderful opportunities I'd been given and how I'd wasted them all. All the loving relationships I'd been blessed with and how I'd lost them all. It reminded me of how I could've made something of myself. How I could have done so many wonderful things with my life. Basically, the whole thing was just a downer.

The holiday reminded me I was alone and miserable with no one to blame but myself. Except for my wife, of course, I could certainly blame her for some of this shit.

Wallowing in self-pity and percolating in poop, I knew I could no longer go on like this. I knew I had to do something and I had to do it fast. So, I quickly consumed three quarters of a marijuana brownie, one hydrocodone, two Ibuprofen, one Xanax and then kicked it all back with a double shot of NyQuil.

"It's beginning to look a lot like Christmas!"

Christmas morning, I awoke early. I was relaxed, restored and well rested. I awoke to discover I'd been given the greatest gift I'd ever received in my life. I got what every man wants but few ever get. I'd been given, "My Freedom!"

I awoke to the realization that I no longer had a wife to support. I no longer had a home to make payments on, insure or maintain. I no longer had a car to make payments on, insure or maintain. I didn't have any children to support. I didn't have any parents to take care of. I didn't have any health issues. I didn't have a job. I didn't have any debt.

Everything I'd known had not been taken from me; I'd been freed of everything I'd known. With absolutely no planning and very little effort on my part I was no longer responsible for anything or anyone except for myself. The universe had conspired to set me free.

At sixty-five years old, I'd been given a "Do-Over" on life and I sure as shit wasn't going to waste it. I was free! I was free to move about the planet!

I didn't know where I was going, but I was going. I was getting while the getting was good. It's not that I didn't have anywhere to go, I now had everywhere to go!

I'd lived the American dream. I had a beautiful wife. I had a beautiful home. I had a beautiful car. I had money and a job I loved. I had everything I ever wanted; but was I happy?

Hell, yeah, I was happy! You're damn right, I was happy! Very happy! Very, very happy!

I was as happy as a man can be, but then the hammer fell. The shit hit the fan. Armageddon! Some bad stuff happened and I lost it all.

When I lost everything I loved, I decided I'd get rid of everything I had. I made a conscious decision to dispose of everything I still owned after the divorce. After all, if I were going to be free I'd have to be free of my "Stuff."

I walked into my double closet and, like a gardener pulling weeds, I pulled clothes from their racks. I packed my jackets, jeans, shirts, shorts and slacks into the back of Christine's car and drove them to the Goodwill store. I sold or gave away my furniture, tools, toys, and art collection.

The more possessions I disposed of the lighter I felt and the easier it was for me to let them go. It soon became a game to me. A challenge to see how much I could get rid of in a day.

I started studying "minimalism" as a lifestyle and the more I learned the more I liked it. I embraced it as a religion, and soon I was on a minimalist mission! After all, if the idea was to get rid of my "stuff," I couldn't be dragging my "stuff" around with me.

Eventually I was free of my "stuff" and ready to travel. I was down to just my MacBook Air, my iPhone and what little I could fit into one carry-on bag. I wasn't going to take anything larger because I didn't want to have to check it at airports.

Everything I still possess will be in that bag and I sure as shit don't want to let it out of my sight where it can be lost or stolen.

Like I said, I'll be carrying my MacBook Air in the bag and it's invaluable to me. It's everything to me. Everything! My Mac is my faithful friend and constant companion.

The doggone contraption does everything for me. It takes care of me. It contains all of the answers to all my questions. It reminds me where I'm supposed to be and when I'm supposed to be there and why I'm there. It organizes and stores all the data necessary for me to live my life.

More importantly, the machine allows me to write. It's the tool I'm using to write; "It's the tool I'm using to write."

My laptop is the only reason I'm able to write this book. That's assuming, of course, these incoherent ramblings actually coalesce into a book.

The idea that I can create stories in my head, tell them to the machine and it types them out for me, is nothing short of a miracle.

When I start a story, I open a new "page" and there is nothing written on it. Nothing. It's a bright, white sheet of pure nothingness. A clean slate upon which I can create. My field of dreams.

I'm an artist and I paint with words.

I begin the writing process by talking to my laptop. I regurgitate an endless stream of consciousness and the computer types my thoughts and my feelings onto the empty page. Misspelled words, nonsensical sentences and irrational thoughts begin floating before my eyes in a soupy sea of white.

The more disjointed, disordered and damaged the words, the more I enjoy the process of writing. It's a puzzle game.

I cut the incoherent sentences up into pieces and shuffle the parts around on the unorganized page. I place nouns, adverbs and adjectives into a semi-rational order and the story reveals itself to me as I move the process along.

I know not what words I may use nor where they may take me. I'm on an adventure; an unknown journey within my head.

Writing is damn difficult and anyone that tells you it isn't has never written anything worth reading.

So, it's time for me to write a new chapter in my life. Time to take the needle off the record, and if you're going to take the needle off the record, then take the fucking needle off the record! Don't pussyfoot around! You can't change your life by doing the "same ol' same ol'" in the same ol' place. It's time to get the hell out of Hollywood and move to Vietnam!

Yes, I'm moving to Vietnam. Why Vietnam? 'Cause I googled it! That's right, I googled it! I started googling places to live and I decided I'd move to Vietnam. I've never been there. Don't know anyone there. Can't read, write or speak the language. It's perfect!

I'd be there already if I weren't stuck here writing about where I was and where I am and where I'm going. I know a lot about where I've been but I don't know much about where I'm going. I just know I'm going and I'm going alone.

I have no choice but to go because there's nothing left for me to leave.

# SUPER IMPORTANT NOTE TO READER

Ever since I was a young, poverty-stricken, malnourished child I have dreamed of one day becoming a successful writer. You can help make my dream come true by writing an enthusiastic review of "I'LL BE ME."

I've always relied upon the kindness of strangers, so:

1. Click on "Write a customer review;"
2. Choose five stars;
3. Write a glowing review (two word minimum);
4. Submit

And BAM! I'm on my way to becoming a best-selling author, getting a movie deal, buying a house in Malibu and partying like a rock star.

I thank you.

You can contact me at jcauerbooks@gmail.com

You can follow me on Twitter at
https://twitter.com/JCAUERBOOKS

You can "like" my author Facebook Page at
www.facebook.com/jcauerbooks

# AUTHOR BIO

As a young man, I only wrote checks. In my later years, I worked in television, movies and advertising, and wrote many memorable commercials. Who can forget, "New and Improved?"

Having always preferred the horizontal over the vertical, I've spent most of my professional career either unemployed or on vacation.

Made in the USA
Monee, IL
19 August 2021